DEDICATION

OF

ANTIOCH COLLEGE,

AND

INAUGURAL ADDRESS

OF ITS PRESIDENT,

HON. HORACE MANN;

WITH OTHER PROCEEDINGS.

YELLOW SPRINGS, O.
A. S. DEAN.
BOSTON:
CROSBY & NICHOLS.
1854.

PRESENTATION OF BIBLES.

At 10 o'clock, A. M., the Board of Trustees, the members of the College Faculty, and invited guests, assembled on a platform at the east front of Antioch Hall, while an immense concourse of spectators gathered in a semicircle below. After music, by the Springfield band, and a prayer by Rev. Wm. Lane, the Rev. John Phillips, having three costly-bound Bibles on the table before him, addressed the President elect, as follows:

Mr. President;

I speak in behalf of the donors of these Bibles. In the name of the Great God, I present them to you as the Constitution of the World. I pray that you, and those under your care, may be guided by their heavenly teaching, and made better by their counsels.

This book is presented by the ladies of Bethany Church, Warren county, Ohio;

This book, by the ladies of Fellowship Church, Warren county, Ohio;

This book, by Messrs. J. & E. Syfers of Jamestown, Ohio.

These you will please to accept for the benefit of the Institution over which you are about to preside.

MR. MANN'S REPLY.

Reverend Sir;

I have been deputed by the authorities of Antioch College to accept these Bibles in their behalf, and to request you to convey their warm and hearty thanks, to the several donors, for a gift so beautiful and appropriate.

Did time and the occasion permit, I might give myself free scope to enumerate and enlarge upon the grand characteristics and prerogatives of this volume of the Sacred Scriptures; I might speak of the venerableness of its antiquity; of the sublimity of its eloquence; of the splendor of its poetry, whose words shine out as though precious stones had been scattered over the page; of its touching pathos; of its precepts and examples of wisdom and truth, and its inspirations of devotion and love; but in this pressure and urgency of the hour, it seems more fitting that I should, so far as I am able, accumulate all excellences in one phrase, concentrate all eulogiums into a single expression; ay, sweep the horizon of time, and of eternity too, gathering their glories into one refulgent blaze, and say, that *it is a book which contains the truths that are able to make men wise unto salvation.*

This book has been subjected by men to many diverse interpretations, and made to speak with most discordant tongues. Rightly interpreted, rightly understood, rightly received, it is confessedly the most precious book ever put into the hands of man. It imparts guidance for life and consolation in death, wisdom for time and hope for eternity. But, falsely interpreted, falsely understood, and falsely received, it has been perverted into the means of inflicting the direst calamities upon the human race,—civil wars, ecclesiastical tyrannies, bloody persecutions, the hatred of Cain, and the cruelty of Herod, and such darkness of the human soul as is blacker than total blindness of the human eye.

For the true interpretation of by far the greater and more essential part of this book, we need only a common degree of intelligence, a conscience void of offence, and that fear of the Lord which is the beginning of wisdom. But for the interpretation of some other parts, all forms of knowledge become needed auxiliaries,—scientific, literary, historical, ethical,—philology, philosophy, mathematics, metaphysics, biography, chronology, jurisprudence, government; in fine, a knowledge of all those departments of the universe, including our own bodies and minds, which illustrate and exemplify the power, wisdom, and goodness of God.

Now, sir, no one knows better than yourself, that a single institution cannot compass all purposes. As our College is not to be a theological or divinity school, we do not propose to inculcate creeds, articles, or confessions of faith; but we do intend, and, with the blessing of God, we do hope, to train our pupils to a practical Christian life, and to make divine thoughts and contemplations become to them, as it were, their daily bread. We mean to administer this College as a literary and Christian Institution, where the mind is to be replenished with knowledge; where the affections are to be trained to duty; where all the faculties of the soul are to be devoted and urged on to the acquisition of truth,—knowing that Truth and God are one,—and where hands shall be made strong and hearts brave, not only in contending for the right, but in contending against the wrong.

To aid us in this great work, we accept your gift, and may the good providence of God so strengthen and illumine our hands and hearts, that in all our administration of the College, we may be guided by His just and righteous laws, and may never fail to hold before our eyes, for imitation, the pure and spotless example of Jesus Christ.

INVESTITURE OF OFFICE.

At 12 o'clock, a procession was formed which moved into the College Chapel,—a spacious apartment, capable of seating fifteen hundred persons,—where, after a hymn by the choir, and a prayer by the Rev. John Ross, the Rev. Isaac N. Walter delivered to the President elect, the charter and keys of the Institution. The ceremony was accompanied by the following address:

Mr. President;

According to the arrangements of the constituted authorities of this Institution, and the duty assigned me on this occasion, I am to present you the insignia of your office. Rome, with her ivory-crested and cloud-climbing battlements, never presented such a spectacle as this. She had become renowned for her deeds of blood in the destruction of life and of the fairest prospects of man. She had Statesmen, Heroes, Poets, Orators, and men who occupied high positions in her ranks, who had climbed to the pinnacle of fame, and dyed their chaplets in the blood of countless millions. She had her Amphitheatres where gladiators fought to satisfy the morbid curiosity of her citizens. But never did she call her people together to dedicate an institution of learning, to instruct her youth in the great importance of cultivating the human mind, to enable her sons and daughters to comprehend the heights and depths of science and moral excellency, which guide men to goodness and to God, and thereby prepare them for their true destiny of greatness and usefulness.

I now present you the CHARTER, as the authority by which this College has been erected and its existence is to be forever perpetuated. I also deliver to you the KEYS of the Institution, which give you authority for full possession of all things pertaining thereunto, and by which you are installed PRESIDENT OF ANTIOCH COLLEGE, and I present you as such to this vast assembly and the world.

Under your administration, may this Institution flourish and grow as the cedars of Lebanon, and as the cloud sends forth rain to fertilize the earth, may the streams of knowledge which go forth from this fountain, enrich the minds of rising generations for ages to come.

This College, sir, is built upon the highest point of land within the limits of our State; the air is salubrious, the water pure, the scenery romantic, and every thing conspires to make it one of the most desirable and healthy spots on the earth. The place on which it stands, a few years ago, was a howling wilderness, inhabited by the untutored savage, who offered up his sacrifice to the great spirit of storms and darkness. Now we have one of the most magnificent structures, for the purposes of education, in our Union.

Under your administration, may the standard of literature and pure morals be raised higher, and shine more brightly here than can be found in any other institution in the world, so that science may go forth as a lamp that burneth. And may the blessings of Almighty God, who upholds the universe by His arm, and feeds the vast family of man from His table, rest upon you in the performance of the duties of the high and responsible station you fill as the presiding officer of this Institution.

Sir, no history tells us for how many years the cloud of mental darkness hung over the aborigines of this country. May this College be as a rainbow over that cloud; and may its light continue to attract and cheer the seekers after truth and the lovers of duty, until it shall shed its radiance on the evening of the world."

MR. MANN'S REPLY.

Reverend Sir;

I know too well the laborious and solemn duties of the office with which you now invest me, not to accept it with trembling anxiety. The best part of my life, and the maximum of whatever humble ability I ever possessed, have been devoted to the culture and well-being of youth. But no day of that life was ever passed, nor any effort of that ability ever made, without leaving upon my mind a deeper and a more vivid conviction of the importance and the solemnity of that work of works,—the development and training of a human soul. For, to what end did God, in the beginning, create the heavens and the earth? why was chaos, "without form and void," reduced to such a majestic order as we now behold, on the earth around us by day, and above us in the "hollow gulf of stars" by night? why were man and woman so exquisitely and wonderfully formed? why did God, out of his own empyrean atmosphere, where wrong had never been, breathe into them the breath of life? and why have the annals of Jehovah been illustrated by so many mighty deeds,—by the mission of Moses, the advent of Christ, and by the sublime march of providential events for six thousand years?—why, I say, has all this been, but for the one all-comprehending purpose, that God might raise up sons and daughters to Himself, from children who had been trained up in the way they should go? God loves the soul above all the rest of the creation; and, therefore, He has subordinated the events of the past eternity to its welfare; and all the sublime annals of His providence are but the history of means and motives to make men wise and holy; and so, by necessity, and not by arbitrary appointment, happy.

Sir, the work of education, always paramount to all others, sometimes assumes a superadded importance. Its appropriate object is youth, and its appropriate duty is to imbue them with the saving predestinations of wisdom and love. Education addresses itself specially to the young, because the young are always ductile and mouldable; while, under our present methods of human culture, the hearts of men fossilize with a rapidity and a flintiness that have no parallel in natural petrifactions.

And a youthful community or state is like

a child. Its bones are in the gristle, and can be shaped into symmetry of form and nobleness of stature. Its heart overflows with generosity and hope, and its habits of thought have not yet been hardened into insoluble dogmatism. This youthful Western world is gigantic youth, and therefore its education must be such as befits a giant. It is born to such power as no heir to an earthly throne ever inherited, and it must be trained to make that power a blessing and not a curse to mankind. With its mighty frame stretching from the Alleghanies to the Rocky Mountains, and with great rivers for arteries to circulate its blood, it must have a sensorium in which all the mighty interests of mankind can be mapped out; and, in its colossal and Briarean form, there must be a heart large enough for worlds to swim in. Wherever the capital of the United States may be, this valley will be its seat of empire. No other valley,—the Danube, the Ganges, the Nile, or the Amazon,—is ever to exert so formative an influence as this, upon the destinies of men; and therefore, in civil polity, in ethics, in studying and obeying the laws of God, it must ascend to the contemplation of a future and enduring reign of beneficence and peace.

But the perils of this region are on an equal scale of grandeur with its powers. Having great varieties of climate, it teems with the richest productions of each; and beneath its fertile surface, lie mines and minerals immeasurable in extent and incomputable in value. Its soil seems to exhale cities; but cities which do not pass, like exhalations, away. Through five great inland seas,—each one of which is large enough to make a geographical reputation for any other country; through the Mississippi and the St. Lawrence,—what would the Roman river-gods have thought of them?—and through artificial channels, capacious even of a larger volume of trade than those natural outlets themselves, it pours forth its abundance, not only for the Pacific and the Atlantic States, but for the eastern hemisphere; and with each refluent tide it receives the luxuries of all the zones. Here, then, is a place to sow something better than dragons' teeth, and to reap something better than armed men; a place to cultivate the arts of peace; to establish a polity that shall protect civil and religious liberty, until the necessity for such protection shall dwindle to a tradition; a place where man shall be trained upon God's plan of development and growth, until to say that he is created in the image of his Maker snall no longer seem, as it now does, like a ridiculous and scoffing falsehood.

When parental fondness gives to a beloved son free access to heaps of gold, the danger is imminent that the son will turn prodigal and squander upon appetites and pleasures what he should have transmuted into knowledge or expended in beneficence. How is it when God is the bountiful Father, and a country, enchanting with beauties above and solid with riches below, is the inheritance given? Ah! if we accept the counsels of God with His gifts, there is no danger, but perpetual rejoicings as of birthdays and bridals; but if we grow proud of the gifts and scorn the counsels, then armed hosts, with quivers full of woes, will beleaguer and assail us. How insane, then, is the common boast, that the population of this or that State increases a hundred per cent., or fifty per cent., every ten years. Suppose Tophet should take a census and find that its population had increased in the same ratio, in the same time; would that be cause for jubilation with those who had fathers or mothers or fellow-beings there? Give to such boast the scorn it deserves. It is the character of a people for virtue and intelligence, and not its numbers, that can give joy or inspire thanksgiving in the heart of patriot or Christian. The reign of truth and righteousness is the only reign from which man can derive happiness, or for which God can accept thanksgiving.

This Western country is increasing in its wealth beyond all precedent in ancient or modern times. It has an annual lake trade of three hundred millions of dollars, and a river trade of four hundred millions, beside its immense traffic upon the Gulf; yet all this, when compared with its undeveloped resources, is only the pocket-money of a school-boy. But without the refining influences of education, wealth grows coarse in its manners, beast-like in its pleasures, vulgar and wicked in its ambitions. Without the liberalizing and uplifting power of education, wealth grows overweening in its vanity, cruel in its pride, and contemptible in its ignorance. Without the Christian element in education, wealth grows selfish in the domestic circle, tyrannical in the State, benighted and bigoted in the Church, everywhere impious toward God. If a poor country needs education, because that is its only resource for changing sterility into exuberance, a rich country needs it none the less, because it is the only thing which can chasten the proud passions of man into humility, or make any other gift of God a blessing.

You have been pleased, sir, to say that in selecting a site for this Institution, you have chosen the highest point of land within the limits of this great State. If I did not misinterpret your manner, you intended to convey some subtle inuendo of an expectation that this local elevation should be typical of an elevation of a nobler kind. To such an intimation words are no fit reply. If answered at all, it must be answered in deeds.

Yet, I trust it is neither vain nor arrogant to express the hope, and even to avow such an intensity of purpose as is some augury of its own fulfilment,—that the waters which pour down from this elevated point toward all parts of the compass, may bear on their bosoms, whithersoever they flow, some influences of sound knowledge and Christian character, which, mingling and co-working with those of kindred and much-valued institutions around us, may help this State to earn for itself the glorious reputation that, though wide in extent, exuberant in resources, and abounding in every aid and stimulant of worldly grandeur, it is yet greater, richer, and nobler in the sons and daughters whom it rears. Abolish knowledge, and Ohio,—the Beautiful, as its name imports,—is again a wilderness, and your children degenerate into new tribes of Shawnees and Wyandots. But perfect education, and your children cannot but rise to an elevation, as yet unknown in your annals, and unprophesied in your hopes. It has been said that Oliver Cromwell was the greatest thing England ever did. Among all the noble achievements of this State, may noble men and women be its highest.

Sir, our enterprise and mission are on the earth, but the fountain whence we draw our spirit is above. I have no hope of any human endeavor which is not founded upon the eternal Law. But for all efforts founded upon that law, I have immortal hope. In that hope, I live and strive.

MR. MANN'S

DEDICATORY AND INAUGURAL ADDRESS.

Gentlemen of the Board of Trustees, and Friends and Patrons of Antioch College;

Let us thank God for the happy auspices under which we have assembled. It is pleasant to the eye to behold the grand and imposing edifice in which we have met; but oh! how much more joyful to the heart to contemplate the beneficent and sacred purposes for which it has been erected. Let us dedicate it to the two great objects, which can never be rightfully separated from each other;—the honor of God and the service of man;—and while we consecrate this material structure to duty and to humanity, let us renewedly consecrate our own hearts to the worship of our Father in heaven, and to the welfare of our brethren upon earth.

But why have these spacious structures been erected? Why this public occasion, and this crowd of eager and anxious spectators? Why these solemn services, and this inauguration of a Faculty, selected from different parts of our wide country, and known, at least for their earnest desires if not for their ability, to promote the well-being of mankind; and why this invocation of the blessing of God upon our enterprise? These, my friends, are momentous inquiries. The answer to them comprehends whatever of weal or woe a human being can enjoy or suffer.

Man is believed to be the last and most perfect workmanship of the Creator upon earth. His organization is most complex and elaborate, and, to the eye of causality, each one of all his faculties has an amazing significance. As a reaper of pleasures, all worlds are his harvest-fields. As a sufferer of pain, every spot in all the worlds may be Guatemozin's bed of fire. His faculties have a range and scope, above, around, below, through what we call immensity; a vision backward and a duration onward, through what we call eternity. He has moral and religious endowments, so that the door of the moral and religious universe, wherein dwell God and all good spirits, stands forever open to welcome his entrance. His spirit can learn its origin in the remote past, and trace its destiny in the remoter future, can converse with its fellow-creatures and hold communion with its Creator, and when it dies here upon earth can rise to immortality in the spirit-land.

But which shall inspire us with the deeper awe, these god-like prerogatives, or the frightful perils that attend them? Our more complicated organization gives scope to more complicated derangements. Give your harp a thousand strings to multiply its melodies, and you multiply its capability of producing discords in a still greater proportion. Send out the human nerves beyond the surface of the body that they may ramify over mankind, in order to partake of their pleasures,—through retrospection over the ancients and through anticipation over posterity,—and a thousand piercing pains shall tell you that these nerves can be conductors of sorrow as well as of joy. Endow the soul with free agency that it may earn a happiness it else could never feel, and by this same gift, you enable it to deserve a remorse it otherwise could never suffer.

Hence we cannot fail to see that the human being may be infinitely the most blissful of all beings within our sphere; or, on the other hand, infinitely the most wretched. All this might be affirmed of man as a solitary individual. But men nowhere live in solitude. They have a social nature which necessitates their union into families, tribes, and nations, as gravitation necessitated the aggregation of chaotic atoms into planets. And in nations, every individual adds a unit to the factor that multiplies all capacities of good or evil. Hence the awful magnitude of a crime when nations put their strength into a wicked institution, or frame a wicked law, or strike a wicked blow. Hence the unimaginable suffering, when a nation turns oppressor and invents and plies the enginery of wrong. For magnitude, for tenacious vitality, there are no crimes like national crimes. Individuals can debase individuals, but governments can brutalize a race. A wicked government makes agony epidemic in space and chronic in duration. It strikes a blow that stuns humanity for ages. Napoleon shortened the average stature of Frenchmen two inches, by selecting all the taller of his thirty millions of subjects and killing them in war. The British government lowered the forehead of the Irish Catholic peasantry two inches, by making it an offence punishable with fine, imprisonment, and with a traitor's ignominious death, to be the teacher of children in school; and by the cruel administration of her cruel laws, she transposed their brain from the intellectual *fore*-head to the animal *hind*-head. False religions have dwarfed the hearts of men in an equal degree by their bloody rites and the shrivelling terrors of superstition. Such, hitherto, has been the current history of the world. Such is the condition, to-day, of the far greater portion of the world.

But can we not find relief from these frightful realities in a cheering anticipation that the curtain is soon to be dropped, and this world-tragedy of ours to be brought to a speedy close? Self-commissioned prophets have been constantly rising up, who have predicted the dissolution of the earth, as though they themselves had made its machinery, and wound it up, and therefore knew how long before it would run down. And this has been done for eighteen hundred years with a frequency and a dogmatism, which perpetual disappointment is unable to check. Even some sober-minded people are haunted with the same delusion. We are so intensely egotistic that we measure other lives, and even the Divine Life, by the hour-glass standard of our own, and hence make a calendar of months and years for the Eternal, as though the Everlasting could grow old. But what do all the wisest and the most religious men tell us, respecting the chronology and the longevity of our globe? The geologist traces back its natural history, age beyond age, and epoch behind epoch, into such far-off periods of the past eternity, that the imagination struggles in vain to conceive the remoteness of its origin. And it is not until science couches the vision, that we see, in these limitless expanses of duration, a scope of time adequate to the grand operations of nature;—time for the diffused material of chaos to gravitate itself into stars; time for frost and flood, for lightning and storm, to break down and triturate the rocks, and fill up the valleys of Niles and Amazons and Mississippis with their rich mould; time for the auriferous mountains to be disintegrated and to cast their glittering treasures along the river-beds and over the vast alluvial deposits of California and Australia, and time for the forests to grow, out of which the coal-fields were made. And when the geologist has brought us over his vast tracts of duration to the present hour, what does the astronomer tell us respecting the durability of that mechanism of the stellar universe of which we are a part? He says that in addition to the revolution of moons around the primary planets, and in addition to the revolution of the primaries around the central sun, our whole solar system itself is sweeping through an immense orbit around some other centre, along a circumference so inconceivably vast that, during the six thousand years since the creation of Adam, the solar group has passed through but about one degree of the three hundred and sixty degrees that make but a single one of its mighty circuits. That is, it has performed, since the creation of the human race, but about one three hundred and sixtieth part of a single revolution. When did ever even an earthly mechanic allow a wheel which he had constructed, to make but one three hundred and sixtieth part of its first revolution, and then stop it forever! The perfect motions of the heavenly bodies allow no friction, no wear and tear, productive of decay. Libration balances libration, and all eccentric movements pass through a cycle and return to their starting-place. It was supposed by Sir Isaac Newton that the moon was straying from its path by slow degrees whose accumulations of error, after long ages, would break up the equipoises of our system, and hence that it would require an outstretching of the Almighty arm to set it back in its place,—as we mortals rectify the errors of a house-clock by moving its hands. But the French astronomer, La Grange, on revising the computations of Newton, found,—what will always be found, when man dares to question

3

the workmanship of his Maker,—that the error was not in the celestial machinery, but in the earthly observer. The moon is faithful to a perfect law of motion, and however it may seem to us for a time to be wandering from its orbit, just as, at the end of each lunation, it might seem to an insect to be waning into final extinction, yet it is as sure to come back to its place in time, as to return to its fulness of orb, — while the error and the insect alike pass away forever.

No part of the natural world seems to grow old. The sun is not shorn of its brightness. The lightning lags not with decrepitude. To the ocean we say, 'Time writes no wrinkle on thy azure brow.' The briny flood distils as fresh water as ever. When this water has risen from the sea on the wings of evaporation, the winds diffuse it over the earth; then the cold condenses it into drops, and gravitation brings it down to the surface; here it nourishes all plants and sustains all life, and flows to the briny ocean again;—thus passing through endless circuits of beneficence; oh, how emblematic of its Maker's love! See too, how the lungs of all the animal world fabricate the aliment that nourishes all the vegetable world. This aliment, the vegetable world analyzes, restores it to healthfulness, and gives it back fitted for the uses of animal life, and thus each is constantly preparing a life-banquet for the other with unfailing reciprocity. What depths of alluvion stand ready to be converted into the varied treasures of Ceres and Pomona; and could these deposits ever be exhausted by transmutation into animal tissues, the decomposition of these tissues would restore them particle for particle and atom for atom, to fill the alluvial basins again. No lightest corpuscle is lost. Nature's workroom and laboratory sweep out no refuse. The multitudinous host of agencies, which God has stationed at every point of His domains,—each a sentinel and a workman too,—never sleep at their posts, and never fail to execute their exact duty in obedience to His unchangeable laws. Age never dims their sight, nor slackens their speed, nor weakens their force, nor abates their fidelity.

Suppose we should see a ship, strengthened against all tempests, equipped with all supplies, provisioned for years, with garments for all zones, with medicines for all diseases, with weapons against all foes, with means for all repairs, even to the re-building of itself, could we suppose that such a ship had been fitted up for the half-holiday excursion of a summer's afternoon!

Now look at the human race, and see how little progress it has made towards the fulfilment of the beneficent design that prompted its creation. It is more than eighteen hundred years, since Jesus Christ lived and taught upon the earth, and yet not one-half even of the present human race have ever so much as heard his name. Only one-third part of this race belongs to what is nominally called Christendom, by which word, if we would imply, what its etymology implies,—"the power or rule of Jesus Christ,"—it is the most extravagant hyperbole ever yet conceived by the mind of man. Look outside of this so-called Christendom, among the vast populations of Asia, of Africa, and of the islands of the sea; take a census of their idol-gods,—malignant, not beneficent divinities; behold their fetichism, their cannibalism, their organization into Thuggery, which is a professed theocracy of robbery and murder; their wars for pillage and man-stealing; see how the natural unity of the race is cut asunder into castes; how the physical and moral laws of God are wrought and woven into all-comprehending systems of superstition and misgovernment; how the body and soul of man have been defaced, blackened, corrupted, until it seems impious any longer to say, that such a race was created in the image of God. Then come within the pale of what calls itself Christendom, which needs a no less ample canvas for the portraiture of its sins. Here, read the first twelve verses of the Sermon on the Mount, and the last ten verses of the chapter in which that sermon is found; repeat the Lord's prayer, and then, as the mariner takes an observation by looking at the heavenly bodies, so let us take an observation by looking at these heavenly lights, that we may find whitherward, according to the celestial chart, this self-called Christendom of ours is tending. Look into the marts of business, the halls of government, the framework of social relations. See how avarice overreaches by law, or plunders without law; how fraud rises to wealth on steps made solid by perjuries; how governments are perverted from the welfare of the governed to the selfish ends of the rulers; how intemperance and licentiousness rage; how vice, though seeking for a hiding-place in our cities, yet reeks into publicity by the malaria evolved from its own fermentation; how the strong man oppresses his brother, and the strong nation makes war upon the weak one; look at the ruffian nations with their foot upon the bleeding breasts of Poland and Hungary, which have ceased to sob but not to suffer; look at Africa's inheritance of bondage;—behold, I say, this panorama of wickedness and woe outspread around us on every side, and then tell me whether it is time for any Christian man to say, "My warfare with iniquity is ended; let me gather my robes around me and lie down to rest."

Now, mute-wondering at this exquisite machinery of the universe which has run for so many myriads of years that are past, and seems capable of running for so many that are to come; and then surveying the immense scale of progress along which the whole mass of the human race is yet to be raised,—first up to the neutral point of zero, by casting off its terrible crimes and degradations, and then above zero by so elevating the spirit of man that, as the Psalmist says, his delight will be in the law of the Lord;—let us lay these two great ideas side by side, and then say whether the time for the earth's continuance seems too long for the work of human elevation.

Connected with this idea of an early dissolution of our earth, another idea is often dimly shadowed forth,—that God will soon have begotten unto Himself a sufficient number of sons and daughters to satisfy all His [illegible] for the human race, and to fill His heavenly mansions; as though considerations of capacity, in regard to His own heart and in regard to the upper courts, must affix limits to the number of the blessed. Oh, the littleness of man's heart, capable of loving only by units and in successive emotions, and therefore contracting the infinite heart of God to the narrowness of his own! Oh, the meanness of man's thoughts, when he takes the foot-rule by which he measures his earthly dwelling, as his base-line of triangulation for measuring the amplitude of the heavenly temple! The music of hallelujahs which will rise to the Father of all from the offspring whom He has blessed will be too loud for any arch or dome save that which Immensity can supply.

How long our race will continue upon this earth we know not. This is a secret in God's keeping. But this we do know, that however long the race, as a whole, may continue, each individual of it makes but a short sojourn before passing onward to his dread account. And one other thing we do know, that, under God, ancestors do predetermine and predestinate the character and fortunes of posterity. A generation modifies the character of its children far more than it does its own. The lateral force of human action, that is, the influence of contemporaries upon contemporaries, is great; but the influence of predecessors upon successors is far greater.

Here, every blow is struck in the direct line of gravitation, and therefore, the mighty laws of nature conspire with human force to give it such weight and momentum as will stamp its impress forever upon all it strikes.

And now, my friends, when I strive to compass in my mind these cardinal ideas: how blissful and how majestic the human race may become, through a knowledge of God's laws and an obedience to them; how tormented and how mean they must also become through a violation of those laws; and how much of that majesty and that bliss, or of that torment and that meanness depend upon us, I am inspired to labor, yea to agonize for their well-being, as though, wherever I can open a channel for human good, or bar up the avenues of human error, omnipotence would pour out its strength through the channel for good, and stand guard over the barriers against evil.

And this prepares me for the remark, that, such is the diffusive nature of human action that no limits can be affixed to the influences which the humblest institution, or the humblest individual, may exert. Some influences act more directly upon one department of human interests and some upon another. It is the high function of a College to act more or less upon all human interests and relations. A college acts upon youth, and hence its influences radiate wherever youth go, and that, in this country, is everywhere. Its responsibilities are commensurate with its influences; and, with a true man, every responsibility is a new incitement to effort.

If then, colleges act upon all the diversified interests of society, by acting through youth, it becomes the most momentous of questions, what do youth need in order to become ministers of good to the world?

Physically, man is born in weakness. He is not the emblem of weakness, but the thing itself. Yet through the organs of his body, he holds relations to all material things. He is adapted to them and they to him; his eye to the light, his feet to locomotion, his muscles to resistance, gravitation and force. If man moves in harmony with the physical universe around him, it prospers and blesses all his works, lends him its resistless strength, endues him with its unerring skill, enriches him with its boundless wealth, and fills his body with strength, celerity, and joy. But woe to the people or the man, who through ignorance or through defiance, contends against the visible mechanism or the invisible chemistry of Nature's laws. Whoever will not learn and obey these laws, her lightnings blast, her waters drown, her fires consume, her pestilenees extinguish; and she could crush the whole human race beneath her wheels, nor feel shock or vibration from the contact.

Intellectually, man is born in blank ignorance. To the infant, all knowledges are a non-entity. A few sensations make up all his consciousness. Yet through his capabilities, he holds direct relation with all the truths and all the wisdom which God has materialized, (if I may so speak,) and incorporated into the frame of nature. The material universe is not matter alone. It is filled with scientific treasures, inconceivable, boundless, endless. Knowledge furnishes the keys by which the apartments of the temple containing these treasures can be unlocked. Hence, whoever will obtain the key of any of these apartments; that is, whoever will acquire a knowledge of the system to which he belongs, can command such riches as Imperial or Oriental despot never dreamed of. Some of these treasures have already been discovered, and they are now enjoyed in the products of those useful and elegant arts which distinguish civilized men from barbarians. But beyond the boundaries of our present knowledge, treasures of yet undiscovered wealth, gorgeous and incomputable, lie crowded and heaped together, compared with which the Gazas and Indies of the past are but the gauds and toys of childhood There they lie, all perfect, beautiful as truth herself, and only waiting for the coming of the great discoverer,—the Bacon, the Columbus or the Franklin of the future age,—to reveal them, and make new benefactions to mankind. Yet this same intellect, by obeying the fiery impulses of appetite and passion may become the engine that sweeps itself and others to ruin.

Morally, man is born on the confines of two worlds;—on the confines of a universe of joy and a universe of woe. As the infant lies unconscious before us, is it not appalling to reflect, that obligations reaching through eternity have already attached to him. He is to live two lives. While the race lives, he is to live on earth, by the influences for good or for ill, which he leaves behind him; and he is to live in another sphere, high or low, near to the Central Perfection or afar off, as his nature shall be unfolded in harmony with or in hostility to the glorious attributes of that Perfection.

Now, it is the comprehensive duty of a College, so far as it can be done by human agency, to equip the youth whom it receives, with terrestrial and with celestial armor to meet the tremendous exigencies of their being. Above all, it is its duty to prepare them to equip themselves.

Listen to me, I pray you, while I endeavor to unfold these three classes of duties, in their order.

All ethical and religious histories, all intellectual philosophies, mourn over the degeneracy of the human heart, and the errors of the human mind. But were all the wrongs and calamities which pertain to the human race, to be classified according to their more immediate relation to the Body, the Intellect, or the Soul, I believe by far the greater proportion of them would be found to proceed immediately from the bodily appetites and propensities. This body of ours in which the soul dwells,—without which, as human beings, we can do nothing and are nothing,—seems not less lost to its first estate of blessedness than either the mind or the heart. Of the three great channels through which depravity sends out its copious streams to corrupt the character of individuals and to blast the happiness of the race, the largest current has its head-springs in the bodily appetites and passions. We weep and bleed at the terrible idea of "Adam's Fall." As to the body, would to God, there had been but one "Fall." But from Adam, through all the generations to ourselves, what has it been but a series of cascades, plunge after plunge, and deep below depth! Would it not be the direst of indignities and blasphemies to suggest that God could ever have created a race, so physically enervated, dwarfed and gangrenous, as ours now is?—not developed but stunted, not beautiful but deformed, not healthy but instead of health, that appalling catalogue of diseases, whose definitions crowd the shelves of the physician's library, and exhaust the copiousness of three languages for their nomenclature. These choleras, these plagues, these pale consumptions, these burning fevers, this taint and corruption of blood, which, after flowing underground for two or three generations, burst up from their subterranean passages to torment the lineage of guilty progenitors;—were all these, do you say, implanted and indigenous in the first generations of men, by God's providence; or have they not all been since generated by man's abuse? Congenital blindness, deaf-mutism, hydrocephalus, insanity, idiocy, did these come normally, through law, or by reason of the most flagrant violations of law? With one-fourth part of the human race dying before they attain the age of one year, what sacrilege to suppose that God said of such a race, "Let us make man in our own image," and then added, "so God created man in His own image; in the image of God created He him; male and female, created He them." Intemperance, gout, scrofula and the through and through rottenness of the licentious man,—did God enact laws which, by their faithful observance, would bear such fruits, in clusters as the vine bears grapes? No! It is impiety to suppose it. Trace back the pedigree of any bodily pain, disease, or privation of sense, and its ancestor, however remote, will be found in some violation of God's physical laws, or in a culminating series of violations, too wickedly great for individual enterprise. Through the temptation of a bodily appetite, man first fell; and all theological schools, and Bible societies, and divine ministrations and ordinances, will never reinstate him in his pristine purity, until the laws of physical health shall triumph, by bringing the bodily appetites and passions within the domain of conscience and religion.

So universal and long-continued have been the violations of the Physical Laws, and so omnipresent is human suffering as the consequence, that the very tradition of a perfect state of health has died out from among men. We are wonted to the presence of debility and pain. Religious men teach us to accept weakness and suffering as the appointed lot of humanity. Hence the conditions of health and longevity are not merely disregaded but ignored, and men of the profoundest learning on other subjects are here ignorant of elements. University professors know how to take care of the solar system, but do not know how to take care of their own systems. I admire the rules of prosody by which Greek and Latin verse flow into harmonious numbers; but I prefer the tuneful pulse which never makes an elision, to any music of classical scanning. I once knew a professor of Rhetoric in an American college, who choked himself to death, at a dinner party, with an undivided piece of mutton. He knew to a semitone the rhetorical proportions in which breath should be sent out of the lungs; but was ignorant of the physiological quantities in which food should be taken into the stomach. Clergymen are forever exhorting us to keep our spirits clean and pure, and then, in their outer-man, they exemplify their teachings by all the defilements of tobacco. They are Boanerges for the advancement of their own sect; but disdain companionship with that sect of the Nazarites who drank no wine. Statesmen and learned doctors debate and discuss the minor questions of Political Economy; but forget that a blight on public health is more pecuniarily disastrous than mildewed crops, and that the most adverse Balances of Trade are less impoverishing than the expenditures for sickness, the non-productiveness of bodily imbecility, and the costs of vice and crime.

I hold it to be morally impossible for God to have created, in the beginning, such men and women as we find the human race, in their physical condition, now to be. Examine the book of Genesis, which contains the earliest annals of the human family. As is commonly supposed, it comprises the first twenty-three hundred and sixty-nine years of human history. With child-like simplicity, this book describes the infancy of mankind. Unlike modern histories, it details the minutest circumstances of social and individual life. Indeed it is rather a series of biographies than a history. The false delicacy of modern times did not forbid the mention of whatever was done or suffered. And yet, over all that expanse of time,—for more than one-third part of the duration of the human race,—not a single instance is recorded of a child born blind, or deaf, or dumb, or idiotic, or malformed in any way! During the whole period, not a single case of a natural death in infancy, or childhood, or early manhood, or even of middle manhood, is to be found. Not one man or woman died of disease. The simple record is, "and he died," or, he died "in a good old age and full of years," or, he was "old and full of days." No epidemic, nor even endemic disease prevailed, showing that they died the natural death of healthy men, and not the unnatural death of distempered ones. Through all this time, (except in the single case of Jacob, in his old age, and then only for a day or two before his death,) it does not appear that any man was ill, or that any old lady or young lady ever fainted. Bodily pain from disease is nowhere mentioned. No cholera infantum, scarlatina, measles, small-pox,—not even a toothache! So extraordinary a thing was it for a son to die before his father, that an instance of it is deemed worthy of special notice; and this first case of the reversal of nature's law was two thousand years after the creation of Adam. See how this reversal of nature's law has, for us, become the law; for how rare is it now for all the children of a family to survive the parents. Rachel died at the birth of Benjamin; but this is the only case of puerperal death, mentioned in the first twenty-four hundred years of the sacred history; and even this happened during the fatigues of a patriarchal journey, when passengers were not wafted along in the saloons of rail-car or steamboat. Had Adam, think you, tuberculous lungs? Was Eve flat-chested, or did she cultivate the serpentine line of grace in a curved spine? Did Nimrod get up in the morning with a furred tongue, or was he tormented with the dyspepsia? Had Esau the gout or hepatitis? Imagine how the tough old Patriarchs would have looked at being asked to subscribe for a Lying-in-Hospital, or an Asylum for Lunatics, or an Eye and Ear Infirmary, or a School for Idiots or Deaf-mutes. What would their eagle-vision and swift-footedness have said to the project of a Blind Asylum, or an Orthopedic establishment? Did they suffer any of these revenges of nature against false civilization? No! Man came from the hand of God so perfect in his bodily organs, so defiant of cold and heat, of drought and humidity, so surcharged with vital force, that it took more than two thousand years of the combined abominations of appetite and ignorance; it took successive ages of outrageous excess and debauchery, to drain off his electric energies and make him even accessible to disease; and then it took ages more to breed all these vile distempers which now nestle, like vermin, in every organ and fibre of our bodies!

During all this time, however, the fatal

causes were at work, which wore away and finally exhausted the glorious and abounding vigor of the pristine race. At least as early as the third generation from Adam, polygamy began. Intermarriages were all along the order of the day. Even Abraham married his half-sister. The basest harlotry was not beneath one of the patriarchs. Whole peoples, like the Moabites and Amorites, were the direct fruit of combined drunkenness and incest between father and daughters. The highest pleasures and forces of the race gradually narrowed down into appetite and incontinence. At length, its history becomes almost too shocking to be referred to. If its greatest men, its wisest men, its God-favored men, like David, could be guilty of murder for the sake of adultery; or, like Solomon, could keep a seraglio of a thousand wives and concubines; what blackness can be black enough to paint the portrait of the people they ruled, and the children they begat?

After the Exodus, excesses rapidly developed into diseases. First came cutaneous distempers,—leprosy, boils, elephantiasis and so forth,—the common effort of nature to throw visceral impurities to the surface. As early as king Asa, that right royal malady, the gout, had been invented. Then came consumptions, and the burning ague, and disorders of the visceral organs, and pestilences; or, as the Bible expresses it, "great plagues and of long continuance and sore sicknesses and of long continuance;" until, in the time of Christ, we see how diseases of all kinds had become the common lot of mankind, by the crowds that flocked to him to be healed. And so frightfully, so disgracefully numerous, have diseases now become, that if we were to write down their names, in the smallest legible hand, on the smallest bits of paper, there would not be room enough on the human body to paste the labels.

I have neither time nor desire to describe to you the pestilent streams, the "Dead Seas" of physical abomination, through which our blood has flowed down to us,—foul as Acheron for the purity of the soul, oblivious as Lethe for the vigor of the mind. Yet the cause and the occasion would refuse to pardon me should I not enforce our obligations to re-elevate the race to bodily soundness, by showing some passages of its loathsome descent. I take one example from Greece and one from Rome,—the two foremost nations of European antiquity. Some passages in St. Paul's Epistles to the Corinthians will be better understood when it is known that *Venus* was the tutelary goddess of their city. She had a magnificent temple on the northern slope of the Acro-Corinthus. This mountain was covered with other temples, dedicated to inferior deities and with the splendid mansions of the opulent. But the fane of Venus rose high above those of all other divinities, and it was enjoined by the Corinthian law that one thousand beautiful females should officiate as courtesans or prostitutes before the altar of this goddess of Love. When calamity impended over city or nation, or when individuals would propitiate the goddess in behalf of private enterprises, they vowed a certain number of courtesans for her service, and such vows were always fulfilled. Opulent men from surrounding nations flocked to a city whose merchandise was licentiousness. Hence ample revenues flowed into the public treasury; and hence that class of men who know no higher law than the law of Mammon and Venus, applauded and sustained her civil polity. Corinth, as may well be supposed, became the most gay, dissipated and corrupt, and so, eventually, the most effeminate and feeble portion of Greece. Would you know something of Athenian manners and morals, look into Athenian literature, especially that of the stage.

For centuries, it was no better in Rome. Matrons deemed respectable, might be seen moving along the public streets, in a state of complete nudity, to witness festivals in honor of the gods, where such spectacles were exhibited as made simple nudity respectable and decent. In the splendid baths, reared by the prodigality of successive emperors, promiscuous bathing could be purchased at the price of a farthing. In crowded theatres, the cry of the audience, "*Nudentur mimæ,*" was instantly obeyed. All of religion that was left, only served to exemplify the amours and licentiousness of the gods.

I cannot repeat what came later, was indescribably worse, sucked vast nations into its engulfing vortex, and has sent down its loathsome influences to corrupt the blood and enervate the brain of succeeding generations.

Every diseased man who bequeaths his maladies to his offspring; every drunkard who rears children from his inflamed and corrupted blood; every licentious man who transmits his weakness and his wickedness as an inheritance of suffering, is another repetition of the Fall of Man.

From such causes, by adamantine laws, and through unalterable predestinations, has come our present diluted and depleted humanity; effete, diseased and corrupt of blood; abnormal, wasted and shortlived; with its manliness so evaporated and its native fires so quenched, that our present world, compared with what it should be and what it might be, is but a Lazar-house of disease, and an Asylum for the Feeble-minded. The imbecile races of Italy and Spain, the half-grown millions of India and Mexico, like river-mouths, are only the foul drainage of ancestral continents, all gushing with fountains of debilitating and corrupting vices.

Then reflect, that, as the number of ancestors doubles at each ascending remove,—two parents, four grand-parents, eight great grand-parents, and so onward,—there are, even at only the tenth degree, more than a thousand conduits of whose united streams each child is the receptacle; and how swollen with the feculence of all transmissible malignities, both of body and mind, must be his blood and brain.

Why then should we wonder that all our animal propensities are represented in our ethics; that Mammon has been the Lycurgus of much of our civil polity, and that a denial of the great law of Human Brotherhood so often finds refuge and resting-place in our popular theology!

It has been somewhat generally conjectured that the early generations had some method of computing time very different from ours, and hence that the patriarchs from Adam to Noah, (with one or two exceptions,) did not, according to the literal record, live to the age of between nine hundred and a thousand years,—afterwards gradually tapering down to between one and two hundred years, at the time of the Egyptian vassalage.* But it is a strong, if not a conclusive argument in favor of a literal version, that, if the race had not been created with ten times more vital force than it now possesses, its known violations of all the laws of Health and Life would, long ere this, have extinguished it altogether. So rapidly had it run down, that, at the time of David,—about half-way from Adam to the present day,—he spoke of the average of human life as only three-score years and ten. Now, ask the Bills of Mortality and the Life Insurance companies what its average is, and they will tell you that in Europe and in the United States, it is but thirty years; and in great cities, but twenty years.

Awful and unspeakable violations of God's laws have done this dreadful work. It is the violation of the laws of Health and Life, I emphatically repeat, which has cut down the years

* With their accustomed disregard of women, the Hebrew historians, with but an exception or two, never mention how old *they* were at the time of their death.

of man to this contemptible brevity and harrows those years with pain; which surrounds the cradle with diseases that spring, like wolves, upon the infant at his birth, and which, instead of the olden days when no child was dead-born, brings such multitudes into the world, who though they may not be dead-born as to breathing, are so as to intellect and heart. A joy that had wings and laughter, once inhabited every joint and vital organ of man's frame. Pain has conquered this festive domain, and turns human breath into sighs.

No other part of the organic world with which we are acquainted has suffered this dire change. Under intelligent culture, the vegetable world is constantly outgrowing itself, in size, beauty and richness. All animal natures thrive, strengthen and surpass the progenitors of their stock, when subjected to the law of their being. Man alone, of all the earth, pales and dwarfs and sickens; begets children, the parti-colored tissue of whose existence is the woof of one disease woven into the warp of another; transmits insanity and gout and consumption and scrofula; procreates blindness and deaf-muteness and those human *fungi*, the brainless idiots; spawns polished imbecility through our cities, which they, by their wealth, send to college, to be converted into pillars of Church and State. And why? Solely because man will break heaven's laws. Because, for the sake of money, or for pride, disease will marry disease, and blood wed kindred blood. Because, when God commanded Adam *to work*, that is, to take some form of exercise; *in the garden*, that is, in the open air, men will not exercise, and will live in dwellings which add artificial poisons to natural ones, and then breathe the virulent compound. Popes and hierarchs send to Jordan to obtain "holy water" for the baptism of their children, that they may give their spirits a figurative cleansing, but will not keep them physically clean with the pure water at their door; and the royal sinner imports a few cubic yards of "holy earth" from Jerusalem in which that body of his may be buried, wherein sin has rioted and wantoned through all his life; — as though they thought the Omniscient could be cajoled into forgetfulness of the difference between "holy water" or "holy earth," and the pure in heart and the obedient in life.

But, besides defying all the laws of God in regard to pure air, cleanliness, diet, exercise, and the selection of healthful occupations and healthful sites for residences,—besides these sins of omission, how numberless are the sins of commission which we commit,—sins which are expelling all manly power and womanly endurance from the race. To say nothing of the stimulants taken in our common morning and evening beverages, (which are no more necessary or useful to enable healthy men or women to perform their labor than a morning dram is for the lark or the eagle, for the buffalo or the leviathan,)—to say nothing of these, the people of this nation annually madden their brains with two hundred millions of gallons of intoxicating liquors; and not only stupefy and defile themselves, but transmit irritable nerves and contaminated blood to their children by the consumption of more than thirty million dollars' worth of tobacco. Of this immense sum, squandered for this foul and abominable weed, it is estimated by Dr. Cole,—an able writer on Physiology,—that the members of the Church of Jesus Christ take five million dollars' worth for their share. It is an indisputable fact that, taking the whole United States together, much more money is expended for the single article of cigars than for all the Common Schools in the Union. Cigars against schools; cigars against the great cause of Popular Education; and Appetite triumphs over Intellect and Morals! And where these natural poisons of alcohol and tobacco are used most freely, the

Church and the Schoolhouse are seen most rarely. I say nothing of opium and other narcotics. And, after quenching still more the expiring embers of vitality that yet glimmer in the race, and corrupting its corruption to a more malignant type, we call ourselves civilized, and,—may heaven pardon the audacity,—Christian. Are those the practices of civilization which honeycomb the bones and leave the muscles sodden, while they irritate the nerves and evaporate electricity from the brain? Is that Christianity which obeys the ceremonial law rather than the eternal; which asks the blessing of heaven upon its food and then gorges itself like a wolf; which offers the morning prayer, but all the day long passes unheeding by the hungry, the naked, the sick and by the prisoner's door? The time will come when men will speak of Christian and un-Christian health, as they do now of Christian and un-Christian character.

For all these ancestral sins, posterity suffers through all its organism, and in every endowment. We suffer for the offences of our progenitors; our descendants will suffer for ours. The self-justifying ancestor may asseverate that his surfeits of viands and wines and his indulgence in narcotics do him no harm, but, three generations afterwards, delirium and gout will shriek out their denial in his great-grand-children.

Now let the man who would fear God and work righteousness survey this subject in its comprehensiveness and its solemnity. As was before said, the larger portion of the crimes against morality and religion,—crimes which savor of the second death,—germinate in what we call the bodily propensities. Intemperance and concupiscence beget the vilest forms of selfishness, beget rebellion against God and the crime of not loving man. Look at the catalogue of offences which the moralist defines in his ethics, or the lawgiver denounces in his penal code,—at once so tropical in their luxuriance and so Tartarian in their fruits;—the murders, the incendiarisms and the nameless and numberless inhumanities of intemperance; the harems of the Musselman and the polygamies of the Mormon, the illegitimate births, the infanticides and the crimes to forestall infanticide; the organized haunts in our great cities where iniquity is transacted by night, as business is transacted in the market-places by day;—and then reflect that these are but random specimens of those offences that come from the lusts of the flesh and the lusts of the eye. Yet these are the crimes that block up the pathway of education, and turn the sweetest persuasions of the Gospel and its most appalling alarms into empty sounds in the ears of men. In view of all this, it is no extravagance to say that our youth need physiological knowledge, as a preventive both against the debilities of ill-health and the ferocities of animal passion, as much as they need literary and scientific knowledge against the calamities of ignorance and superstition, or religious training for the love and service of God.

However well-intentioned men may become under the influence of literary and religious institutions, yet when the bodily organization is weak, the power of virtuous effort is proportionably enfeebled. In a languid frame, benevolence and piety themselves degenerate into revery or barren contemplation. Sickly men dare not take the field, and wage battle with their satanic foes. If money-changers invade the temple, they cannot scourge them out. If wicked men build distilleries or kidnap Africans, they can only write a moral tract or sing a pious song, and let distiller and kidnapper go on. Next after heaven, the brave heart of Martin Luther had its reinforcements from his strong frame. All along the life-way of a pure-minded but feeble-bodied man, on the right-hand and on the left, his path is lined by memory's gravestones, which mark the spots where benevolent enterprises perished and were buried, through lack of physical vigor to embody them in deeds.

> "'Tis then, a painful sense comes on,
> Of something wholly lost and gone;
> * * * * * *
> Of something from our being's chain
> Broke off, not to be linked again."

If it be a solemn duty to keep the spirit pure, as a sanctuary for the Most High; if heart and soul and mind are to be devoted to the service of God and of our fellow-men; then who can overstate our responsibility to keep the body,—through which alone and by which alone, the highest achievements of practical heroism can be won upon earth,—in the robustest working and militant condition. Oh, if piety, like the army, kept a sick-list, what a populous hospital it would show! Well did the Apostle say "Let not sin, therefore, reign in your mortal body, that ye should obey the lusts thereof." Well did he urge his followers onward by telling them that "every man that striveth for the mastery [in the race] is temperate in all things." Well did he exhort all who called themselves by the name of Christ to present their "bodies a living sacrifice, holy and acceptable unto God." And well did he set forth, what was perhaps the greatest of all his achievements: "I keep under my body, and bring it into subjection, lest by any means when I have preached to others, I myself should be a castaway."

Now think for a moment what mankind would gain, were they relieved from early decrepitude, and from the weakness and bondage of earlier bodily ailments. What elasticity would be given to muscle, what vision to mind, what pinions to genius. What can the consumptive man do in felling a forest, by the side of the hardy pioneer,—the one exhausting his strength on a sapling; the other, mowing the trees into windrows. The tall man stretches up his hand and plucks the fruit, without an effort, which the child would perish before he could reach. It is just so with the tall mind compared with the short one. No combatants are so unequally matched, as when one is shackled with error, while the other rejoices in the self-demonstrability of truth; yet when virtue contends with vice for the extirpation of social abuses, or for the advancement of great reforms, how often do the strong-bodied reprobates vanquish the weak-bodied saints. In all the higher departments of invention and discovery, in the soarings of genius, and in the exultant aspirations of sentiment, all well-organized and healthy persons rise, as by natural buoyancy, to the sublimities of an upper sphere, whither imbecility, or mediocrity of strength, with all their strivings, can never soar.

Half of what passes among men for talent is nothing but strong health. I do not here so much refer to the sound man's power of mastering truths by intuition, which the sickly arrive at only by long pains-taking, as to his ability of persistance in holding on to any work, after weaker hands are forced to let go; his power of continuing the chase for a noble prize, after weaker limbs faint, or of stretching the vision on and on, after common eyes swim and darken.

Besides, about the same amount of time must always be lost in coming to the age of maturity, whether the available period of subsequent life be cut down to twenty years, or extended to a hundred.

I often used to wonder why the moderns, with all our accumulations of power derived from the sciences; with such an expansion of the useful arts, by which, through the medium of machinery, we train the forces of nature to do the far greater portion of our work, and with a consciousness every way so much richer than belonged to antiquity;—I have often wondered, I say, why the moderns, with these incalculable advantages, are comparatively so little in advance of the ancients. Not only in the sayings of the wise men of old, but in the excavations of Pompeii and Herculaneum, in the decipherings of Champollion, and in Layard's exhumed wonders of Nineveh, there are such proofs of wisdom, of genius and of skill,—such intuitions into the very heart of things,—as give a transient plausibility to the old hyperbole, that there is nothing new under the sun. With the experiences and discoveries of all past times treasured in our books; with our alliance and co-partnership with the powers of nature; with the beacons of ancient error to warn, and the illuminations of ancient wisdom to direct, our advance beyond all our ancestors ought to be immeasurably greater than it now is. The only solution of the painful problem is this: that all our immense advantages have but a little more than indemnified us for the appalling degeneracy of our physical strength and our mental intuitions. The improved external world of nature and art have been almost cancelled by the deteriorated internal world of vigor and insight.

I must dwell upon this topic no longer now, unexhausted though it be. Yet when I ponder upon the wealth of human happiness that lies folded within it, I am almost tempted to call upon the student to leave his learning, and the philosopher his science, and the clergyman his theologies, and first teach men how to obey the laws of God in their physical frames;—how to glorify Him in their bodies, as an accompaniment, if not a pre-requisite to glorifying Him in their spirits.

Oh, how beautiful is the ever-changing and ever-renewing beauty of Health!—the marmorean repose of infantile sleep; the singing gladness of childhood; the exultant and sometimes wayward impulses of youth, intoxicated and bewildered by varieties of joy; the firm, rightonward march of manhood unbarbed by an arrow of pain, and uncrippled age at last, venerable in its serene and lofty front;—how beautiful are they all! Less beautiful is the clear-springing fountain with its flower-adorned brink; less noble the mighty river cleaving its mountain-barred passage to the deep, and less reflective of all the glories of heaven, its outspreading and calmer current as it lapses and dies into the sea!

A second grand want of the human being, in this world of ours, is the development of his mental faculties, with skill to use them. There are two ways of making the Mind more powerful. The first is by improving the bodily constitution, or physical organization of the race, so that, with more healthy bodies we may have stronger minds; and the second is, by giving all the skill and efficiency we can to such mind as there is; whether it be the miserable mind that belongs to a weak race, or the powerful mind that belongs to a strong one. The first is the work of Physiology; the second, of Education.

Of the necessity of Mind, what need have I to speak? I might as well speak of the necessity of air to the bird's wing, or of water to the fish's fin. Almighty mind guides the universe. As to this earth, just in proportion to the development and culture of man's intellect, he participates in that guidance;—knowledge enables him to lay his hand upon the great machinery which God has constructed, and to direct its movements for his own benefit.

Hence, in order to be fitted for our present sphere, we need Mind,—the clear-shining and far-shining of the luminous intellect. If we would find new constellations in the heavens, or discover new features in stars already known, we demand a telescope of greater space-penetrating power. No longings, no night-watchings, no aspirations, will ever enable us to see one inch beyond the capacity of our glass. Give me a "larger eye," says the astronomer, and I will reveal to you another rank of worlds marshalled behind those whose shining hosts you now behold. Rear stronger minds, says the lover of light and truth, and they will lift up the race to sublimer heights of dignity and power. In this way, we shall obtain thought-producing, instead of thought-repeating men. Mind is immeasurably more valuable than any form of material wealth. For one such man as Arkwright, or Fulton, or Sir Humphrey Davy, the world could afford, if it had them, to give a hundred Californias, and pay them down. One such man as Whitney is worth more than all the Common Schools of New England ever cost. If the mere doctrine of chances, if what we call mere fortuity, would turn up one such Christian patriot and statesman, as John Quincy Adams, once in a hundred years, it would reward all the bravery and pay for all the perils of the May-Flower.

Now, on this topic there are two or three great principles to be brought into view, in whose light the pathway of human duty becomes radiant.

In the first place, there is no increase of absolute truth in the universe, and there can be none. The number of minds that know truth may be indefinitely increased, but there can be no more truth to be known. All truth preexisted in the Divine Mind. The creation of the visible universe, with the formation of the countless orders of beings that dwell in it, did not create truth; it only displayed it. It only made those things objective, in the splendors of creation, which before were subjective in the Divine Mind. The race knows vastly more now than it ever knew before, and will doubtless go on redoubling its stores. But He who was always Infinite cannot be more than infinite now. He who was always Omniscient cannot know more in the future eternity than He did in the past. We speak of men, as making new and wonderful inventions and discoveries. We cannot speak so of the Deity. Truth, therefore, is not progressive; though finite beings may be forever progressive in acquiring truth.

Ever since the creation of Adam, the heavens have been as full of starry glories as they will be to-night. The distant constellations shot their arrows of light into human eyes as they do now. Why then, were the power and glory of God so long belittled and vilified by the universal conviction that the sky arched itself but a few furlongs over our heads, and that all the wealth of the heavens, as was supposed in the time of Ptolemy, consisted in but a thousand stars? Why were the moons of

Jupiter, the fluid rings of Saturn, the orbs of Uranus and Neptune, and the vast islands of light that move in their appointed spheres through the immensity of space, whose beams with all their lightning speed, are supposed to have been millions of years in reaching our earth,—why were all these grandeurs and glories of Jehovah a non-entity to man! There they stood, rank behind rank, in vaster circles, refulgent through all the ages, as at present,—a fit frontispiece to the volume of God's goodness and power;—but human eyes beheld them not, and human hearts were not lifted up to God by their majesty and splendor. The race waited for the great minds that should lay open these starry depths of heaven. The minds came, the depths were laid open, and the celestial light blazed down upon us to attest the power and beneficence of the Creator, and again to make all the sons of God shout together for joy.

It is so in regard to all things. In all philosophies, in all theologies, in all principles of whatever kind, there are now just as many absolute truths in existence as there ever will be. There they exist, more valuable to man than zones of gold, sweeter in affections than unfallen Eden, sublimer than any Patmos yet revealed to man; and the problem which we have to work is, to prepare the men who can discover these more glorious truths, just as men prepared the telescopes by which the pre-existent stars were discovered. The truths whose shining faces no mortal hath yet seen are no less real, they will be no less freighted with blessings when they come, than those by which we have been already gladdened and improved. But they lie beyond the frontier of our present knowledge, and therefore, as yet, are useless to mankind. We need the minds, and therefore, we must rear the minds, which can push forward this frontier of knowledge, so as to bring these truths, with all their benefactions, from the further to the hither side of the line,—from the barren possibility of being enjoyed, into actual, realized enjoyment.

To suppose the contrary of all this would be to suppose that we had already exhausted the wisdom which God incorporated into the frame of nature and of ourselves; and, with our nutshell capacities, had laden dry the ocean of omniscience. No! for while the world stands, the topmost heights of science will never be reached; there will be no last Avatar of genius.

What the human mind has already achieved, by availing itself of the bounties of Nature, has been often said and sung in eloquence and poetry. Man wanted more labor than he could himself perform, and then, not by superior strength but by superior mind, he domesticated and trained the animals,—the ox for strength, the horse for fleetness. These were not enough, and so he enslaved his fellow-man. But intellect saw mightier powers in the elements than in any muscles of beast or slave; and now gravitation strikes our blows in the ponderous hammer, and steam cleaves the billows, or rushes across the land, to bear our burdens or ourselves. The winds once swept by the savage, useless as the fleecy clouds they wafted on their bosom; but mind has trained them to bear the bark of the explorer to every part of the earth and to waft the commerce of the world. The lightning once came only to terrify and blast; but now, it executes costly embellishments in the shop of the artificer, and bears messages of intelligence and affection, wherever the telegraphic wire is stretched. Man prepares and arranges a few wheels, and by His agents of air and water and fire, God turns the machinery by day and by night, to supply our persons and our dwellings with the fabrics of comfort and elegance. To form the strawberry, the peach or the grain of wheat, the elementary atoms of which they consist, traverse continents and come from every zone. By what we call the laws of chance, how few of these atoms would ever meet and mingle to form our nectarious fruits, or our nutritious harvests. But the agricultural Art summons its infinitesimal hosts,—the mineral from the earth, the gases from the air, the water from the clouds, the light from the sky; leads them through all the subtle and mysterious channels of vegetable growth, and elaborates them into all the golden harvests of the year. What fulness of granary and storehouse, what freights for ship and car, come from agricultural knowledge,—that is, from Mind,—where once the barrenness of earth and the barrenness of ignorance spread a common solitude. Mind, too, has the still nobler power of improving itself, and of spreading a glory of health and strength over the whole body with which it works. Thus, through navigation and printing, through the steam-engine and the telegraph, through agriculture and chemistry, through vaccination and chloroform, has intellect lifted mankind a little way out of barbarism. We see the riches of those apartments in God's temple which science has already unlocked. Through Physiology and through Education, we must rear the intellects than can unlock inner apartments filled with the more gorgeous treasures of the infinitely benevolent Giver.

The ancients were so religiously impressed with the displays of elemental forces, that they personified them into divinities. In their theology, the earth became populous with gods and goddesses. Each river had its river-god. Apollo shone in the sun. Boreas howled in the northern blasts. Jupiter threatened in the lightning, and struck in the thunderbolt. The ancients advanced the elements into gods by deifying their attributes.

Anglo-Saxon egotism has gone to the opposite extreme. We boast of conquering and subduing the forces of nature. What the ancients worshipped as gods, we speak of as captives and slaves. In our self-complacency, we talk of imprisoning the elements to make them do our bidding. We boast of turning the lightning into an errand-boy, of using gravitation as our pile-driver, of tasking rivers and winds to grind in our mills.

How different from all this is the view of the Christian philosopher! How much more *filial*, that is, how much more religious, in us; how much more honoring to God, to look upon all the mighty energies of nature as His gracious gifts to His children; our allies and not our foes; as never griping to withhold, but always standing open-handed to give, whenever we will ask them in the language of science,—the only language they understand. They were created to supplement our weakness, to lend their velocities to our tardy limbs, to work for us when we are weary or asleep. Indeed, is it not both the grander and the truer view, to regard the mighty organisms of nature as only part and parcel of the human organism,—as only more gigantic limbs, more ponderous and far-reaching and swift-moving instruments with which to carry on the super-eminent work of elevating and ennobling the human soul? Man has been called a Microcosm,—a Little World,—as though he were the epitome or adjunct of the earth, instead of the earth, with all its mighty energies, being his adjunct or instrument. Are the powers of nature any the less our powers, because there are some of them which we have not yet learned how to use? What part of the body of an infant, does its soul, at the first, know how to use? Not one. Its limbs lie flaccid and inert. Its liveliest senses make no response to light or sound. It is only by slow degrees that the informing spirit takes possession of its tenement, and begins to work its wondrous machinery. It just turns the eye, lifts the hand, moves the foot. Now it walks, now runs, and anon, it climbs mountains and circumnavigates the globe, levels forests to let in sunshine and cultivation, rifts open granite hills for cities and temples, and scatters libraries, galleries and fleets from its fingers' ends. In the same slow way, and in perfect analogy to the infant's progress in getting the use of its own limbs, is the infant intellect of the world now diffusing itself outward through the frame of nature, and getting the use, one after another, of its tremendous energies. Already, the Titan begins to feel his strength. Already, he uses gravitation as his heel of iron and fists of porphyry. The lightning is his nervous fluid, which darts along new fibres of electric wire, to write out his will through the machinery of his outer fingers, a thousand miles off; or to shout in the ears of half a million of sleepers that their city is on fire. Beyond the shortsightedness of his bodily eye, nature supplies the laws and means for a telescopic eye, whose lens is not of a six line, but of six feet diameter; and lo! what an Infinite of glorious worlds greets his enfranchised vision. The corporeal eye cannot see in darkness; but what is the magnet but another eye of his, from which no thickest cloud or dazzling sunlight can hide the pole-star. He cannot see corpuscles and monads; but under the microscope, atoms before invisible start up into new worlds

4

of vegetation and zoölogy. Surpassing all fictions of winged chariots, he is borne across seas and lands in chariots without wings. Whether he wills to have fruits from the tropics, or spices from Araby, or diamonds from Golconda, the winds are his breath and waft them whither he will; and at his volition, a Crystal Palace becomes a show-case for the wonders and beauties of a planet. The flying images of all visible things, with which all sunlight is filled, he catches at will, by the Daguerrean art, and preserves them for his own. With his vocal organs, he can address but a few thousand men, and, in an instant that voice dies away and is gone; but with his other multiform tongue, the Printing-press, he speaks, and as his glittering words fly forth on wings of wind and fire, they are seen by millions of men; and whatever of wisdom is spoken is graved on tablets of stone for the Ages. The rivers and the fires are his strength; they wheel his ponderous machinery, or hammer in his Cyclopean forges; and, like the blood in his own veins, or the warmth in his own bosom, they rest not from their service, day nor night. The chemical atoms, classified and assorted by his intellect, and mingled and medicated into unerring chemical proportions by his agricultural skill, come together not only to diversify the outward world with the riches and beauty of corn and fruit, but to begin the great processes of being transmuted, through the wonderful alchemy of Life, from marl and metal and rock, into muscles and lungs and brain. Nay, in some things, man seems to do more than to own and employ the energies of nature, as though they were part of himself. From his full sensorium, he forces thought and activity into the brute materials around him. If a chronometer or a calculating machine cannot think, yet how many thoughts are there in them! What is that assemblage of inventions which crowd the halls of Patent Offices, but exemplifications, how the soul of man is working outward into nature, endowing it with the capacities of life, and organizing its massive bulk, fibre after fibre, into more than Archimedean forms of skill, and more than Briarean arms of strength? Nor is he forbidden to extend his power over Life itself. At his will, the valleys are covered with cattle, or the air is filled with birds; or, as by a recent and almost creative discovery, the rivers of a continent swarm with new piscatory life.

And thus, I say, the soul of man is feeling its way outward, beyond his own body, into the body of nature. By his compelling thoughts, acting through mathematical, chemical and organic laws, he is preparing new organs of sense and new instruments of power; getting a larger eye and a mightier arm and a lightning swiftness of foot; learning to use crushing weights and upheaving expansions, and to multiply ten thousandfold the means of subsistence, of culture and of moral elevation. His spirit, after penetrating and vivifying his own frame, penetrates and vivifies the frame of nature around him.

"Spiritus intus alit, totamque infusa per artus,
Mens agitat molem, et magno se corpore miscet."

And lo! in achieving this work of might and splendor, the noblest fruit of all is the mind's own simultaneous elevation to dignities and grandeur unknown before. However far the soul penetrates into the deep recesses of the earth; however far it sets back the canopy of the heavens, revealing vaster panoramas of the glory of God; with whatever of guidance it directs the elements, or incorporates its thoughts into insensate matter; or into whatever new forms of power and beauty it organizes and embellishes the earth;—with all this amplitude and adornment, it first enlarged and enriched itself. Self-improvement must precede all other improvement. Whatever miraculous creations have been scattered over immensity by the Divine Hand, all must first have existed in the Divine Thought. The Maker is always greater than the fabric made. And so it is with men. Whatever new wonders of art or genius or utility are yet to enrich the world, all must first have their prototypes and models in the gorgeous chambers of the brain.

As each generation comes into the world devoid of knowledge, its first duty is to obtain possession of the stores already amassed. It must overtake its predecessors before it can pass by them. The parents may be Magi for learning; their infant child will not know his alphabet; not know that he needs one. The former may be able to give nations a dowry of wisdom and prosperity. The latter must first learn how to keep himself out of fire and water. In learning there is no exclusive heirship. No last will and testament can bequeath genius; and the son of a Bacon may be a dolt. In our time, it is no small labor to bring the children up to the knowledge of their fathers. But we are not to stop where we are. We have but just got a foothold on the infinitude of God's knowledge and wisdom; just trod upon the outer verge of His illimitable realms. No natural impediment forbids our turning what is now Divine Knowledge into human knowledge. We may ascend

Pisgahs after Pisgahs, and enter Canaans after Canaans, yet forever see before us new Pisgahs to be ascended, and Canaans flowing with the milk and honey of a diviner wisdom, to be made our own.

To accomplish these high purposes, the College is demanded. It is our duty not only to see that the present stream of knowledge brims its banks, but to make it overflow those banks, and spread richer alluvion over wider intervals; and, for every league of its future course, to pour in mighty confluents of new discoveries, from the right hand and from the left, that its current may grow deeper and broader forever!

But *can* coming generations add indefinitely to previous acquisitions? All the realms of thought shout an affirmative reply. It is a saying attributed to Euclid, that there is no royal road to learning. This adage, I must deny. Knowledge is communicated and acquired indefinitely better and faster in one way than in another;—through such a language as the English, than through such a language as the Chinese; by the synthesis of elements, than through the analysis of masses; by means of the eye, rather than of the ear; by building with the solid masonry of reason, on the rock-bottom of intuition or principle, instead of the castle-build ing of memory. Dugald Stewart said that a young man could now learn, in two years, all the mathematics known to the ancients. It is most fortunate that he has not to unlearn what they thought of astronomy, or meteorology, or physics in general. There *is*, then, a royal road to knowledge; and educators will find one more right royal still,—that is, one shorter and more firmly trod;—and therefore, so far as it regards knowledge, we should erect our statue to the god Terminus, face forward, and set it on wheels. The immigrant who trudges a-foot, with his pack on his back, or trundles the barrow that contains all his earthly goods, may as well deny that there is any better method of travel or of transport than his, while the earth-vibrating locomotive at his heels shakes the falsehood out of his mouth.

God's heart is full of new mechanical and new physical blessings for the race. He only waits for the fullness of time when Physiology and Education shall produce the *Men* with talent and genius worthy to be the medium of their transmission to mankind. God knew the weight of the atmosphere and the law of gravitation; He saw this western continent; He knew how books could be printed, how cloth could be woven by machinery, and how lightning would run through iron, as well in the time of Solomon and Socrates, as since; but, in the order of His providence, He had to wait for Torricelli and Newton, for Columbus and Faustus, for Arkwright and Franklin, before He could bless mankind by the bestowment of that knowledge. In the same way, He waits for us, through a knowledge of the laws of Physiology and Education and an obedience to them, to rear the new men for the new blessings. Man's ideas of the earth are yet to be as much changed by chemistry as his ideas of the heavens have been by astronomy. Chemistry will yet beautify the earth as much as astronomy has glorified the heavens.

For augmenting the aggregate amount of intelligence and mental power, in any community, the grandest instrumentality ever yet devised is the institution of Common Schools. The Common School realizes all the facts, or fables, whichever they may be, of the Divining Rod. It tries its experiments over the whole surface of society, and wherever a buried fountain of genius is flowing in the darkness below, it brings it above, and pours out its waters to fertilize the earth. Among mankind, hitherto, hardly one person in a million has had any chance for the development of his higher faculties. Hence, whatever poets, orators, philosophers, divines, inventors or philanthropists, may have risen up to bless the world, they have all risen from not more than one millionth part of the race. The minds of the rest, though equally endowed with talent, genius and benevolence, have lain outside the scope of availability for good. These millions, with the exception of the units, have been drudges, slaves, cattle;—their bodies used, their souls unrecognized. Ah, nowhere else have there been such waste and loss of treasure, as in the waste and loss of the Human Faculties. All spendthrift profusions, all royal prodigalities, are parsimony and niggardliness, compared with the ungathered, abandoned treasures of the human soul. As civilization has advanced, perhaps one child in a hundred thousand, and, in more favored nations, one child in ten thousand, has been admitted to the opportunities of knowledge. Forthwith, the men capable of constructing the institutions or the engines of human improvement and adornment appeared; and in numbers, too, far beyond the proportionate share of the constituencies from which they sprang. But if, instead of striking the fetters of prohibition from one in a hundred thousand, or from one in ten thousand, those fetters are stricken from all, and incitements to exertion and aids to self-development are supplied to all; then, immediately, quick as water gushes from unsealed fountains, Shermans rise up from the shoemaker's bench, Beechers come from the blacksmith's anvil, and Bowditches and Franklins from the ship-chandler's and the tallow-chandler's shop, and a new galaxy shines forth over all the firmament of genius. These are truths which the uneducated nations do not understand;—truths too, which the caste-men, whether of birth or of wealth, do not wish to understand.*

It is in this way that the Common School awakens talent, and sets it in motion. And when once the inward impetus of native talent is aroused, you may as well attempt to stop the whirling of a planet, as to arrest the possessor of that gift. Then comes the function of a College, to guide, replenish and speed it on in its immortal career.

---

* "To the more advanced half of Christendom, the prizes voted at the London Fair, [the Crystal Palace Exhibition of 1851,] by the juries and by the Council of Presidents were *one hundred and four*.

"To the less advanced half of Christendom, the prizes voted by the same tribunal were *two*.

"To the totality of non-Christian nations, composing two-thirds of the whole human race, *nothing*."—*Report of the French Commissioners to the Industrial Exhibition.*

And here open upon us the great utilitarian views of education, as a preliminary to its higher and nobler spiritual functions. As we survey the present condition of the world, and look forward to the well-being of posterity, we find problems to be solved, which virtue alone can never solve, which piety alone can never solve; but for which only knowledge, talent, genius, that is, intellect, can furnish the solution. The coming generations are to be fed, clothed and sheltered, — not miserably, as the aborigines were, by the precarious chase, or the earth's spontaneous growths; not in skins and caves; but with abundance and certainty, with comfort and elegance. The heathen humanity heaped up in all our great cities, six stories high,—in Edinburg, I have seen it eleven stories high,— the wretched inmates of the Irish mud-house, of the Hottentot kraal and of the Tartar tent, are to be provided with a decent home for every family. Mankind at large are to be educated, not a few beloved Benjamins, but all the sons,— AND ALL THE DAUGHTERS TOO,—and all inconceivably above our present standards. The libraries of which our cities are now proud, must exist in all our towns. Apparatus for explaining the wonders of nature, museums, cabinets, gardens, such as now enrich our colleges, must be the possession of our schools. The means of mental and moral growth must come and stand around our children and youth, unasked and unpurchased, as air and light now come to their cradles. All heathen lands are to be civilized and Christianized; and what we now call civilization and Christianity are to be purified and elevated into forms indefinitely higher than at present prevail.

Now what vast expenditures of money, what a long series of instrumentalities, what an immense apparatus of natural means, even before we come to the use of moral means, does such a catalogue of enterprises, or rather of necessities, imply! Judging according to present standards, and only including what is absolutely essential to the well-being of the body, to the training of the mind and the culture of the heart, it may be safely affirmed that spontaneous nature and spontaneous intellect, — that is, uncultivated nature and uneducated intellect,—do not furnish, and never can furnish, one ten thousandth part of the supplies indispensable for such a race as its Maker needs not to be ashamed of,—needs not to repent Him that He had ever made. I speak literally. I desire this to be taken as a statement, unhyperbolical and uncolored, that, without the dynamic forces of nature acting through some form of apparatus or machinery and doing the work of the world; without the chemical forces of nature, acting through the art of agriculture and producing the sustenance of the world; and without the schoolhouse and the college, with kindred seminaries, developing the mind of the world; there would not be, even according to our present low standards, one ten-thousandth part of a sufficiency, either of bread for the body, or of bread for the soul, to enable the human race to appear decently in any part of the universe that can call itself respectable. Without both natural and mental resources, such as can alone come from a knowledge of those laws which God has inwrought into the frame of nature and of ourselves, and without some good degree of obedience to them also, the whole human race would have to be abandoned, in commercial phrase, as a total loss. Where, then, are the other nine thousand, nine hundred and ninety-nine parts of the things, indispensable to raise us above our present constructive civilization and constructive Christianity, to come from? They are to come from the human intellect! God gave a few fruits, the berry and the root, for food; he gave the fountain for thirst and the cave for shelter, and then, for the sustenance, the self-protection and the self-aggrandizement of the race, he gave the rest in the faculties of the Human Mind! Marvellous complement of human weakness and ignorance; miraculous resource of infinite and never-ending bounty!

Why were not the aborigines who so lately traversed these regions, as well equipped in all the necessaries, comforts, conveniences and luxuries of life, as we are? They, not less than we, trod an earth, whose ribs were covered ten feet thick, with alluvial fatness. For them, as much as for us, incomputable hoards of metal and mineral had been laid up in subterranean chambers. The same winds swept across the lakes, and the same streams poured down the valleys, then as now. They also, were endowed with the same faculties of intellect. But they had never learned the agricultural arts by which the centillions of centillions of primary atoms, which were lying at random in the ground, or running vagrantly in the streams, or floating uselessly in the air, could be summoned together into the gluten and farina, the albumen and phosphorus, into the hues and forms of all our varied plants and bulbs and grains, all medicated for the stomach, flavored for the palate and beautified for the eye. Their undeveloped mind had never taught their unskilled hand, to make that other hand,—the mechanics' chest of tools,—which has ten thousand fingers on it, to cut and saw and bore and shape and polish; nor that other hand, which has ten thousand wheels for fingers, which can card and spin and weave and knit and sew; nor any other of the Briarean hands or arms of genius, which can do the work of the world, whether in the shop or in the mill, on the land or on the sea, from polishing a needle to forging the shaft of a steamship; from turning a gimlet to tunnelling a mountain; from cutting a thread to reaping a prairie; from measuring a field to measuring the heavens.

The American Bible Society is said to have printed, during the thirty-seven years of its existence, nine millions of Bibles and Testaments. Now reflect, that this number, great as it may seem, is but about one copy for every one hundred souls on the globe; and as, in the meantime, more than an entire generation has passed away, if we allow ten years as the average existence of a book, before it is worn out or lost, it would leave less than one copy for every four hundred souls. In the seven hundred Public Libraries which now exist in these United States, there are only about two millions of volumes, which is but one volume for every twelve persons in the Union,—instead of fifty or more volumes for every person, as there ought to be. Think then what a work it must be, not only to prepare the Sacred Scriptures for all the children of men, but to scatter books, as they must yet be scattered, like autumn leaves, over the earth; to dot the five continents with schoolhouses, as New England is dotted, and to supply them with all the higher institutions of learning, better than New England is supplied; to turn iron, marble and oak, to turn wool, flax and silk, to turn carbon, hydrogen and nitrogen, into abundant materials for human shelter, raiment and food; and thus to furnish, not scanty necessaries only, but all comforts and embellishments to every household on the globe; and so relieve the slave, the serf and the hunger-goaded freeman from so much of toil, as is incompatible with culture, elevation and enjoyment.

Now, for all that has been done in these various ways to improve the condition of the race, intellect, teeming with its observant and combining powers, has been the pre-requisite. Without the saw-mill and the nail-factory, how could our houses be built; without the spinning-jenny and the power-loom, how could our clothes be supplied, and without the power-press and the paper machine, how could our newspapers and our books be printed?

How worthless in themselves, are the materials from which glass is made, but how beautiful the product! Nero is said to have given six thousand sesterces for two glass cups. So late as the time of Queen Elizabeth, there was but one pair of silk stockings in England, which were owned by the queen and were valued almost like the jewels in her crown. The first printed Bibles sold for five hundred or six hundred crowns. Now the glass cups and the silk stockings can be possessed by all, and the Bibles are twenty-five cents apiece. All these improvements came from intellect; and, for more improvements, we must have more intellect, which is just as produceable a commodity as any in the market. Steam navigation now earns for this country more than a hundred millions of dollars a year. Other Fultons will make it earn other hundred millions. So ten yards of cloth can be manufactured where one is now manufactured; ten bushels of grain raised for one that is now raised; and fifty books made for one book, and all better than before. Stronger and swifter machines are yet to be made for traversing the earth, and nobler instruments for exploring the heavens. And when this is done, the epics, the histories, the philosophies, and the ethics will be as much better as the machines.

In this way, all the grand institutions and instrumentalities which are held to be the crown of our present civilization have come into being. The magnetic needle led to universal commerce; railroads came out of steam; universal popular education from the art of printing and paper-making, and without roads and bridges, a representative republican government, like that of the United States, would be an impossibility. Means, too, are to be increased faster than men increase, so that the multiplied millions of posterity may have better fortunes than their fewer ancestors. And all this vast and demiurgic work,—I might almost call it a *theurgic* work,—is to be done through the inventive and discovering faculties of man, drawing for instalment after instalment upon the mighty reservoirs of power and wisdom, with which God, for this beneficent end, has filled the earth and the elements. Or rather, as I before suggested, the intelligence of man is yet to pervade the earth as it now pervades the body, and to command the forces of nature as it now commands its own limbs, and to wield gravitation, wind, fire, tide, caloric, electricity, as it now uses hands and feet, or eye and ear. Here is a theatre where the dignity of our nature can be vindicated, and the greatness and goodness of Jehovah displayed. To those who are to train the youth of both sexes for their impending work, I say, in the words of Revelation, "He that hath ears to hear, let him hear."

But besides the physical and the intellectual, there is the moral nature of man,—the coronal part of our being. To this department, belong the awe-inspiring ideas of duty and destiny, and the awe-stricken sentiments of wonder and adoration. Here our contemplations rise from the mighty genius who can draw down lightnings from the lower heavens, to the hallowed genius who can draw down sanctities and beatitudes from the upper heavens. It is through moral and spiritual power that the rivers of thought and feeling are to be turned, as men now turn the rivers of water.

The moral and religious part of man's nature is the highest part. Of right it has sovereignty and dominion over all the rest. Some of our faculties were bestowed for a temporary purpose. This was given for an eternal one. If the appetites govern, they bring the whole physical system to sudden ruin. But if the spiritual nature, enlightened by the intellect, governs, then the bodily system runs rejoicing to its goal. The whole scheme of creation,—man and nature,—

was based upon the supremacy of the moral faculties. Let but the laws of God be understood and obeyed, and justice and love will reign over all the earth, and man will be restored to his Eden of happiness.

As indications of the supremacy of the moral faculties, and as a measure of their success, we use the terms Civilization and Christianity. But these terms are most vaguely used. If subjected to the least rigorous definition, they can import nothing less than *a Knowledge of the laws of God and an Obedience to them.* It matters not, in any good sense, what men profess; it matters not what books, or institutions, or revelations they may have inherited; the stern question forever recurs, *Do they know the will of God and do they obey it?* Judged by the standard of Knowledge and Obedience, how far is the best nation in the world, at the present time, authorized to call itself civilized or Christian?

In regard to the physical part of our being,—our bodily appetites and propensities,—I ask the Christian physiologist, what part of the world there is, where men know and obey the laws of God, in this department of their nature? Alas, my friends, pain, disease, debility and brevity of life, all personify themselves as giants, to vociferate, *There is no such place.* In all that pertains to the bodily health and soundness, whether of ourselves or of our children, ninety-nine hundredths of all the best communities in the world, are still heathen in their daily practices and life. Those appetites which they have in common with the brutes, they do not govern; but they allow the appetites to govern them. The first distinction between an irrational and a truly rational being is this: the former seeks, primarily, the pleasures of food; the latter, the uses of food. The one consults appetite and indulges; the other consults reason and abstains. Among our people, I mourn to say, in eating and in drinking, and especially in using alcoholic or narcotic substances, appetite is the god they worship. Natural, or rather unnatural desire, uncontrolled by reason, determines their conduct, and thus predetermines, to a great extent, their own future health and that of their children. Reason and conscience alike teach that if any of the forth-springing impulses, that wake to spontaneous activity within us, ought first to be bridled and reined in, the despotism and audacity of our lower nature ought so to be. Until all concoctions for the titillation of the palate, until all stimulants for the excitation of the brain, are made subordinate to the soundness of the stomach and the purity of the blood;

until reason and conscience shall rise in majesty above the subject propensities and bind them, like hounds in the leash, and until men shall have reference, in their matrimonial connections, to the physical laws of hereditary descent, they have no right to call themselves civilized or Christian, in their treatment of the body. They either do not know, or, knowing, they do not obey this part of the laws of God.

I grant, there is indefinitely more now than formerly of what calls itself refinement and elegance, in all our domestic life; but alas, how little of it has any reference to the four cardinal conditions of our normal state, — to the four Evangels of the body, health, strength, beauty and longevity. And if the care of the body is more refined than formerly, that refinement is mainly Sybaritic. If its pleasures have been enlarged, the enlargement is mainly in the direction of voluptuousness. But this change from gluttony to epicurism is of doubtful utility; because I believe it to be quite as easy a task to bring a man forward from beastly gluttony to a healthful dietary, as to bring him back to it from idolatrous epicurism. As to the bodily appetites and propensities, then, the best nations and communities on the earth can, as yet, advance no claim to true civilization. It is not an object with them, to study how to make the strongest and most healthful bodies, as it is to study how to make the fastest-sailing clippers, or to raise the largest oxen or swine. Even the highest circles of society, as they call themselves, are often seen glorying in their shame; for, in what quality of dignity or decency, does the publication of a "Bill of Fare," with all its profusions and prodigalities, after some metropolitan feast or entertainment given by duchess or queen, excel a cannibal's display of bones, after a human barbecue?

In regard to the body, there are four proofs that we are not yet a civilized people: First, men sacrifice health to wealth, instead of wealth to health, and do not seem to know that the surest way even to get money, is to get a good body and brain to work with. Second, while there is an almost universal desire among parents to educate their children better and to leave them richer than they themselves were, and while the more advanced communities make strenuous and combined efforts for these ends, we see only occasional and transient indications of a desire to confer upon those children more health and strength, more power of endurance and the prospect of a longer life, than belonged to the parents themselves. Thirdly, notorious indulgence of appetite and propensity, even in the gross forms of intemperance and licentiousness, if combined with great talents, hardly presents an obstacle to political promotion, while living, or to extravagant eulogies after death. Practically, the great talent, instead of aggravating the guilt, is held to atone for its commission. And fourthly, while, with our abounding worldly prosperity, new temptations are constantly springing up around us, new moral restraints to confront and oppose them, do not rise up within us. Hence, the new sources of enjoyment are abused, rather than temperately used. Prodigality triumphs over frugality. The wealth is shamefully expended on low tastes and gratifications, which was designed to be nobly consecrated to art, affection and charity.

And is it any better in the moral part of our being? Here we have two infallible tests of human character;—two infallible tests by which to determine whether we know and obey the will of God. The first has reference to man. It is the test of Human Brotherhood;—do we love our neighbor as ourselves? Among whatever people the law of caste prevails, or the fact of caste without the law; that people has no right to call itself civilized or Christian. I use the word *caste*, because, as an anti-social term, it is generic, and embraces all forms of human selfishness. A people tolerating caste do not love their neighbors as themselves; they do not do to others as they would be done by; and therefore, whatever religious rites or devotional forms they may practice, they fail to practice the eternal law. The animosity of race, whether it be of the Jew against the Samaritan, of the Turk against the Christian, of the Chinese against the outside barbarian, or the European against the African, is as contradictory to the spirit of Christianity as water to fire. Where either exists, the other necessarily non-exists. This is one test.

The other test is derived from the other great commandment, and is no less decisive: Whereever complete religious toleration is denied; that is, where men are accepted into favor, or treated with aversion, because of the religious opinions they have formed, and not because of the honesty or dishonesty, with which they formed them, there the offender has no right to arrogate civilization or Christianity for himself. The command to love God with all our powers necessarily involves the absolute freedom of those powers; otherwise, it is not rational and spontaneous love, but factitious and constrained; not the result of vital, conscious action, but of machinery. Christ came to make men free in thought as well as in spirit; and whoever would fetter men's thoughts, would fetter their limbs if he could. We are bound to judge men by the integrity of their lives, rather than by the accuracy of their logic, and an unintentional error of the intellect is never to be compared with a conscious dereliction of the heart. That would be as erroneous as to compare a mistake in metaphysics with the crime of blasphemy.

A people who tolerate great national sins are not entitled to be called Christian, or morally civilized. Is it said that sin gets organized into the framework of society, so jointed and articulated that it cannot be removed but by demolishing the structure of society itself? I answer that there is not one of the dishonesties of trade, or the profligacies of politics, or the bigotries of faith, or the inequalities, that is, the iniquities of feudalism or caste, that would not be hurried into oblivion in a single year, if a majority, or even a considerable minority of the community were really Christ-like or Christian. The most sensitive musicians could more easily live amid a perpetual thunder of discords, than a truly Christian body of men, amid the sights and sounds of misery that could be prevented and of sins that could be quelled. The old history stands for a universal truth; and not the ancient Sodom alone, but any Sodom could be saved by ten righteous men.

What a comment upon the churches of Jesus Christ it is, that not a single one of them, throughout all Christendom, constitutes an exception to the rule, that, where pecuniary obligations are concerned, a legal bond is the universal substitute for confidence in the bondsman's personal integrity.

It is in the sphere of the intellect alone, that men are becoming truly civilized. Here they have learned some of the laws of God, as expressed in nature, and they do obey them. And how magnificent are the rewards. How the crude substances of nature are changed into comfort, beauty and blessedness. How our knowledge of the stars enables us to traverse the earth and to navigate the seas, without losing our way. What myriad spectres of superstition, the knowledge of nature's laws has exorcised from mountain and grove, from cavern and glen, from midnight and twilight. As we descend into the globe and bring up its agricultural and its mineral treasures, we learn how deep down in its bosom the earth loves man. From the first and few rudimentary lessons, which the intellect has learned, and learned to practice too, from the great volume of God's will, have proceeded the vast multiplication of our comforts, embellishments and means of progress, just as naturally as a bird comes out of an egg. Such is our reward for knowledge and obedience in one department of God's laws.*

And by what means has the intellect obtained such vast pre-eminence over the other departments of our nature, in learning what the laws of God are, and in reaping the rewards of obedience to them? In modern times, it has pursued two methods as yet almost peculiar to itself.

In the first place, keeping its eye ever open

* Principally, however, thus far, the laws which the intellect has learned are of the utilitarian kind, — such laws as increase possessions, and the power to use the forces of nature. Their contributions to physical and moral well-being have hitherto been indirect and collateral. For instance, in our great cities, many private mansions have lately been erected, at a cost of not less than a hundred thousand dollars each, in which not the slightest provision has been made for ventilation, any more than if their occupants were non-breathing animals, and could, (if I may use the phrase,) *hybernate* all the year round. The successful business-man or banker hires the builder and the upholsterer to lavish the most they can for ostentation and pride, adding here and there some excrescent ornament, to show that the owner has taken the tour of Europe. But with all their wealth they do not show a gleam of knowledge how to convert even a tenth per cent. of their prodigality into the means of health for themselves and their children.

and its mind ever receptive, it has sought earnestly for new truth, instead of expending itself to defend hereditarily-descended opinions, and keeping its eye shut and its ear stopped against all suggestions that do not square with old theories.

And second, the lovers of this kind of truth do not split themselves up into schools or sections; one, for instance, to maintain the Neptunian, and one the Vulcanian theory of the earth; or one to contend for the material, and the other for the vibratory hypothesis of light; but they have all come together, as in the French Academy of Sciences, in the Royal Society of Great Britain, and in those Associations for the Advancement of Science which have lately been organized both in Europe and in this country, where each member submits his views to the friendly criticism of all the rest, and to the tests of truth, and still remains in fellowship and in friendship for the discovery of new truth, with perfect toleration to hold any diverse opinion, on any point. Had the inquirers after the truths of nature divided themselves into sects and classes, one to maintain the faith of Hutton, and one, of Werner; one to fight for the theory of Newton and one for that of La Place, and then gone back to their closets or their pupils, to denounce all new discoveries and vilify the discoverers; had they looked backwards to keep all systems of philosophy where they were, instead of forwards to enlarge and perfect those systems, and to modify, (as new truths always do,) our views of the old truths;—had this been done, the whole glorious region of Natural Science, and of the Useful and Elegant Arts dependent upon it, would now be substantially where it was in the time of Lord Bacon; and men, sunk in hateful depths of poverty and meanness, would still be imprisoning Galileos as they have excommunicated heretics. And how admirably does this common and cosmopolitan love of truth operate. When Agassiz or Faraday or Arago discovers or announces a new truth, joy thrills, like electricity, round the whole circle of devotees to science. They know that these men were not bred in any narrow school; they know that the minds of these men were never absorbed into any *ism* or *ology;* they know that these men have no motive of pride, or class, or title, to uphold the wrong or repel the right; and therefore, after hearing the announcement with candor, and examining it with care, with one accord, they adopt the discovery into the great republic of truths, where it will be a sovereign forever. So, rightly and rapidly to interpret the will of God, even with a revelation in our hands, will demand the entire forces of the human mind,—all co-operating and none thwarting,—and before the will of God can be obeyed, it must first be known. Oh, when will mankind be as zealous for new moral and religious truth, as they are to invent a new reaper or gold excavator, to discover a new fossil in the earth, or a new planet in the sky!

Hope dawns even here. The analogy is most instructive, and, in one respect, most cheering, between the civil or political condition of mankind, in the Dark Ages, and its spiritual condition, at the present day. Then, the people of Europe were broken up into petty clans and feudatories, just as what we call Christendom is now broken up into sects. The chiefs and barons of those times made constant war upon each other, so that conflagrations consumed their cities and battles devastated their plains, exhibiting the self-same spirit, politically, which is now exhibited, theologically, between Catholics and Protestants, the Greek Church and the Latin, or Churchman and Dissenter. Then each feudal lord had his castle for defence and his armed retainers for offence; as each sect now has a Periodical for its armory, and itinerant proselyters for the invasion of foreign territory.

Then, there was no competition for higher agricultural science, or for improved mechanical arts, or for more healthful architecture, or for a truer education of youth, as there is now no competition between the different denominations, for practising honesty in trade, or recognizing the law of God in politics, or giving charity to the wretched, or doing justice to the wronged.

But by-and-by, indicating the first dawn of a better political day, a few neighbor chiefs began to form friendly leagues and alliances, for mutual protection or defence, in precisely the same manner as those different religious bodies in our day, who have doctrinal affinities, have combined to defend their own denominational territory, or to invade that of a borderer. Such partial unions and compacts were the harbinger of civil and political reforms, then, as they prophesy religious reforms now. After this first step, private wars soon began to cease; men dared to venture abroad from under the covert of walled towns; the travel upon highroads became less unsafe; intercourse extended and commerce grew up; until at length, natural rights came to be so far recognized, that men could live in the open country without armed protection, and without danger from robber and assassin. The religious world is now in the very first stages of this progress. Its organized bodies occasionally form alliances with each other to subserve a common object; but even yet, no individual can venture beyond the pale of his own faith, without as great danger from the shots of his own camp, as from those of the enemy. But as the sects emerge from their present hostilities, they will find all theological strifes to be as injurious to the moral well-being of mankind, as the feudal wars of barbarous times were to their temporal interests. Then will all Christians come bodily or spiritually together in "World's Conventions," or in "Year Books" of Theology, or in the "Philosophical Transactions" of benevolence, to investigate the laws of the human soul, and the conditions of human welfare; as scientific men assemble now,—in a temple whose doors open towards all points of the compass; — and Christian love will work that grandest of all miracles, — that miracle for which all other miracles were wrought,— the conversion of belligerents into brothers, and the reign of Peace on earth!

But these great reforms in corporate bodies and in communities will never be achieved, until private morals are brought into closer approximation to the standard of the Gospel. Surely, it is the most appalling fact in all our annals, and it ought to make every parental heart palpitate with alarm, that the College, where the youth of our country must be sent for the higher culture of the mind, should ever expose them to a depravation of the heart. And yet it is an opinion not uncommon, and would to God I could say, not wholly unfounded, that, as young criminals learn new lessons in crime when sent to our public prisons, so young men lose purity of character and contract habits of vice, when sent to College.

Is it not amazing, when the grandest fact in all the phenomena of nature, with the grandest principle in all the sciences which the student learns, is, that we are in a universe of immutable laws, that effect follows cause with unerring certainty and resistless force, and that we must reap the harvest whose seed we have sown; yet that the same student should ever make the mistake, or be allowed to make the mistake, that the faculties and the fortunes of his lower nature or of his higher nature can ever be the subjects of chance; that his fate is not fastened to his motives by rules, as adamantine and indissoluble as those by which the tides heave and the planets roll. In all departments of Botany, pupils are taught to believe, and they do believe, that upon the constitution of the seed, upon a healthy germ and a vigorous growth, depend all beauty of the flower, all succulence, flavor and nutrition of the fruit, all robustness of stalk or trunk, and all promise of transmitting the virtues of a better stock to subsequent growths. They are also taught to believe, and they do believe, that all this holds true throughout the entire realm of zoölogy. Why should they fail to see that it all must be eminently true of anthropology,— that is, of themselves? Why should they be taught, that, in dynamics, the power must be greater than the inertia, and in statics, that the resistance must be equal to the pressure; and yet not be taught, so as to feel a far livelier consciousness of its truth, that the quantum of energy must exceed the maximum of obstacle, or no heroic enterprise will ever be achieved, and that moral principle must grow as temptation grows, or we are swept to ruin. As the lightest particle of spray thrown up by Niagara obeys the law of gravitation as much as the rushing cataract itself; as the mote that floats in the sunbeam is swayed by the planets, as they themselves are swayed by the sun, so each lightest thought which the mind consciously harbors, and each feeblest emotion to which it yields consent, must alter the character of the soul itself, and must change the altitude of its sphere through all the stages, even of an eternal ascension. Every virtuous deed which a man performs brings an angel to his side to counsel and to bless, but with every crime which he commits, a new Nemesis is born.

To render the cultivation of the intellectual nature beneficial or even safe; nay, to save it from being baneful, it must be accompanied by moral education. As warp and woof when woven together, make a texture a hundred fold stronger than either taken by itself, so must moral education be inwrought with intellectual to give strength to the character of youth. The very constitution of our nature teaches us that these two departments should never be disjoined. United, they are allies; separated, they often become foes. In a man devoid of morals, the intellect often acts as a mighty pander to all the evil passions. In a man devoid of intellect to foresee consequences and weigh probabilities, a blind devotion to one good object makes havoc of whatever other good objects may stand in its path. The inquiry has sometimes been made, which is the more necessary to the world, intellect or the moral sense? We might as well inquire which is the more necessary to our natural life, air or food. Doubtless a being of both infinite intelligence and infinite goodness, can see no difference between the expedient and the right; for whatever is right must, in the long-run, be expedient; and whatever would, in the long-run, be inexpedient, could not coincide with the right. But as the knowledge even of the most knowing man, in regard to the common events of life and the consequences of conduct, can penetrate but a hand's-breadth into the future, a faculty became necessary which should, like the magnet, always point to the pole-star of duty, however deeply that star might be obscured, either by the brightness of prosperity's day, or by the darkness of adversity's night. Hence, we were endowed with the faculty of conscientiousness, which tends towards the right by an innate polarity, and admonishes us to embrace the true and spurn the false, long before we can obtain a ratification of its dictates from the conclusions of reason, or the results of experience. It is as absurd, and it is a grand part of moral education to make it appear to be as absurd, for a man to discard the injunctions of his conscience, as to deny the evidence of his senses, or the inferences of his reason. What should we think of a man who, in spite of his senses, should dash himself against rocks or edifices as though they were non-existent, should step from precipices as though there were no law of gravitation, or should drink molten metal as though it were his natural beverage? Yet during infantile life, before the senses are trained, this is precisely the way in which children act. What too, would become of a man who should use the multiplication-table backwards in his business; or who should construct optical instruments on the principle that light naturally moves in curved lines, or who should demand as a geometrical postulate, that a part is equal to the whole? Yet children see nothing of the absurdity of all this, until their reason is developed; until they have profited by months and years of instruction. And no less incompatible with our higher nature, no less hostile to our true destination, is it, to revolt against conscience, to turn a deaf ear to the promptings of benevolence, to stifle feelings of veneration for whatever is holy and true, than to discard the demonstrations of geometry, or abjure the evidence of eyes and ears. But common education has not yet acted on this philosophy. And hence the imbeciles, the idiots, in morals, have been far more numerous than those in intellect. The old Romans who augured the fortunes of individuals and of the State from the flight of birds, or the entrails of animals, were idiots in philosophy, just as parents who rear their children in habits of self-indulgence instead of self-restraint, are idiots in education. The man who cheats in trade is not merely a cheat, he is a fool; and the mean pleasure of the knave who passes off a counterfeit bill is the shabbier counterfeit of the two. The supposed sagacity and cunning of the plot by which the diplomatist circumvents his adversary, is the very trick by which the devil is circumventing the diplomatist himself. When Benedict Arnold betrayed his country because he wanted money to minister to his vices, he was on no higher an intellectual level than the monkey who excoriates his throat with scalding water, because he is thirsty. The man who anxiously avoids the shadow of a granite post, but dashes against the post itself, is not a whit more witless, than he who fears the appearance of doing wrong, but is not afraid to do the wrong he thinks will not appear. When Lord Chesterfield counselled hollow-hearted politeness,—advised the forms of courtesy and graciousness instead of the things themselves,—he must have seemed to any superior order of moral beings, as silly as the ape, who puts a wig upon his head, and expects to be reverenced as a judge. When Spain kindled the fires of the *auto-da-fé*, and stretched victims on the rack, those fires dried the blood out of her own heart, and through the crippling and mangling of others' limbs, she herself has never since been able to walk erect. The bigotry of the Roman Pontiff, which forced Galileo to deny the motion of the earth, did not stop that motion, but it did stop the intellectual activity and progress of all Italy, so that she has never been able to set herself in motion again. The so-called statesman, who barters human liberty for money or for office, the priest who hopes to save souls by Jesuitical pretences, are but the figures in a puppet-show played by a fiend. Every wrong done is a weight which the wrong-doer throws above his head, which is as sure as gravitation to fall back upon, and wound or crush him. Where now, in the world's estimation, or in their own, are Constantine, Cæsar Borgia, Cardinal Wolsey, Henry the VIII, or the partitioners of Poland?—gibbetted, hung upon a gallows fifty cubits high, the eternal winds of execration howling curses forever through their bones, an abhorred spectacle to God, to man, ay, and to themselves! At the Judgment-day, even Satan himself, all concreted into falsehood as he will be, will be seen to be still more of a fool than a liar!

It is so of all oppression, of all unjust wars, of all crimes national or individual. God created the universe upon the principle of the supremacy of the moral law, and it would be easier for mankind to walk on their heads or breathe in vacuity than to subvert this moral order of creation. And all these propositions are as capable of demonstration as any theorem in mathematics. I know there are cases, where men, who see the fatal consequences of wrong, still do wrong; but the cases are many to one where men do wrong because they have never seen its adamantine connection with fatal consequences. The law of right is incorruptible and eternal, and children can be taught this law, as they can be taught geography or astronomy. But if children are not as faithfully and as anxiously indoctrinated into this law,—I do not mean into the words that define it, but into the thoughts and sentiments that constitute, and the deeds that perform it,—as they are into the Rule of Three, or latitude and longitude, then the moral nature does not enjoy an equality of privilege with the intellectual nature; and, until it does enjoy such equality, there are no principles known to us, either in human actions, or in the divine government, from which we can expect the highest moral results. Were God to give us such effects without their related causes, He might as well give us any other effects without their related causes,—growth without nutrition, wisdom without thought, or happiness without love; — that is, He might as well annihilate His whole system of Cause and Effect.

The cultivators of the silkworm have discovered different kinds of food for that insect, by which they can color the material from which the silk is formed, red, blue, or otherwise, in the body of the animal itself; so that the beautiful cocoons when spun from its stomach, shall not have been dyed into a given hue, but have grown into it; shall not have been colored with this or that color, but created of it. So let it be with the moral aliment the child receives. Let truth be the nutriment, and devotion to God the honey-dew of his life. If man does his part of the blessed work of education, early and wisely, we are certain that God will crown his labors with infinite blessings hereafter.

With every wise parent, the character which a child brings with him out of college is of more consequence than everything else which he brings. How natural to the parental heart is the exclamation of Jacob, "If I be bereaved of my children, I am bereaved." Yet the groans of father and mother at the natural death of a child are hymns of joy and exultation, compared with the quenchless fires of their agony at his moral ruin. There is a calm and celestial beauty in the lifeless form of an infant, who has died in its innocence; but with the ghastly features of one whom, not age, not disease, but hideous vice has brought to the coffin and the shroud, there come surges of woe which beat back all approaches of consolation. The more I see of our present civilization and of the only remedies for its evils, the more I dread intellectual eminence, when separated from virtue. We are in a sick world, for whose maladies the knowledge of truth and obedience to it, are the only healing. Oh, if the literary institutions of our land would sanctify their ambition; and, instead of an earthly rivalry to send forth great men, would provoke each other to the holy work of rearing good men, then would they be doubly rewarded both by greatness and goodness, such as they have never yet imagined. Referring to the comparative worth of scholarship and morals, Montaigne says, "We know how to decline virtue, but we know not how to love it." I believe I can speak for all my colleagues in the Faculty, and certainly I do for myself, when I say, in regard to the morals of the pupils who shall be folded under the wing of this Institution, as Jacob said, after having wrestled all night with the angel of God, "I will not let thee go, until thou bless me."

In endeavoring thus far to unfold the merits which pertain to the three great departments of education, — the Body, the Mind and the Heart,—the course of the argument has restricted me mainly to their effects upon individuals as individuals, — to their power of bestowing strength, beauty and pre-eminence upon the particular man or woman who possesses them. I have not described their more slow and indirect, but grander action, in what they will do for nations, as nations, and for the race as a race. Over and above what education does for the men and women whom it personally blesses, there is a collateral and a magnificent result in what it does for mankind at large. Besides the private power and enlargement which it confers upon its possessor, it also confers a corporate or common power and enlargement upon all. The Republic, in which there are many learned and wise men, must be almost as much elevated by their elevation, as the learned and wise men themselves. It is this diffusion of benefits, this common and public function of education, which re-acts with such amazing effect upon individuals. If the weight of the atmosphere immediately surrounding a few persons were to be doubled, the general effect would be imperceptible; but double the weight of the earth's atmosphere, and all acoustic apparatus, all wind-borne vehicles, all pneumatic machinery, would be suddenly endued with new and vaster energies. So when the common stock of knowledge is enlarged, all men are enlarged; because, if gigantic ideas are given even to a pigmy, the pigmy becomes a giant. Though the inventor of the steam-engine and the discoverer of the telescope may have intended to invent and discover for themselves alone; yet they could not help giving the strength of ten thousand arms and the vision of ten thousand eyes to all mankind; and when an inspiring thought glows up, like sunrise, in the soul of genius, a new sun is lighted up in the firmament of all men's consciousness, and a ray out of the eternal Effulgence is poured over the world.

It has been demonstrated in a late work,* that an inevitable necessity has presided over the order in which Human Knowledge has had its birth; that there is a lineage in the sciences, so that the modern could not have preceded the ancient, any more than Noah could have been the father of Adam. But the idea which I here insist upon, goes further: there is not merely an order but a momentum, in human advancement.

* The Theory of Human Progression.

The perfecting of the simple or rudimentary sciences hastens the progress of the complex, so that the highest of all the known spheres of human thought, — political economy, jurisprudence, government, education, theology, ethics,— must emerge with accelerated velocity from former darkness into future light. This law of momentum is as obvious in human progress, as in mechanics. When the *vis inertia* is overcome and a headway is attained, all impulses are cumulative, and men must compute their advance by a double reckoning, — by adding each new accession of velocity to the *constant* of velocity already attained. It is no longer a mere movement of gigantic minds urging forward the race; it is a movement of the race itself, imparting new speed even to the gigantic minds themselves, and rousing the common mind, which otherwise would be torpid, to activity.

And if mankind have already derived such vast benefits from the intellect,—from that only part of their nature, where as yet, they have systematically begun to comply with the two divine conditions of all human progress,—finding out the Laws of God and then obeying them,—what unimagined magnificence and glory must await the race, when the search for this knowledge and the practice of this obedience shall be set down and recognized as the established Programme of the world's exercises!

For, still more self-expanding and self-propelling will be the blessed influences of a public or common virtue, than of a public or common intelligence. The contrast is infinite between virtue and vice, not only in nature, but in function. Vice is always selfish, bestowing, it is true, a certain amount of mean and sordid and short-lived gratification upon the actor alone, while it shoots arrows of pain at every one else; but virtue diffuses eternal joy and beneficence upon actor and object, upon spectator and auditor, down to the end of the generations. Hence, while known vice, from the nature of things, can have but one defender or apologist, — the vicious man himself, — virtue, from the same nature of things, has all mankind on its side except the one vicious man whose machinations it thwarts.

Hence the two instruments for abolishing error and wrong from the earth, and for heralding in the true Christian Era among men, are Truth and Love, (which are the synonyms of Knowledge and Obedience;)—both kinds of truth, natural as well as spiritual, and both kinds of love, love to man as well as love to God. Truth shows us that the commands of God, our duty to our fellow-men and fidelity to our own highest interests, never conflict, always coincide, and that either one necessarily imports or signifies the others. Love annihilates no elementary attributes of being, but, in selfish natures, it changes the working of them all, so as to make the practice of truth the highest delight. The first conceptions of natural and moral Truth, accompanied by the feeblest glimmerings of Love, drove three hundred thousand false gods out of Greece. Before those powers, Jupiter, who sat throned in Rome for a thousand years; to whom her armies vowed their vows for all the myriad victories of their battlefields, and to whom the senate decreed their thanksgivings for conquest, was left without a worshipper in all his temples, and was consigned to the realm of Fable forever. Those heaven-commissioned ministers invaded the ancient forests of Germany and expelled Thor and Woden from the halls of Valhalla. They redeemed Britain and Gaul from the bloody dominion of the Druids, and our own continent from the false theologies of Indian and Aztec. And thus must Christian truth and love, purged and redeemed from error and selfishness, spread abroad their reign of benignity by conquering the conquerors of the world; by subduing cannibalism, fetichism, idolatry and the bloody rites of superstition; by abolishing pestilence, famine, war, intemperance and poverty; and especially that all-comprehending misanthropy, the Law of Caste, which includes within itself every form of iniquity, because it lives by the practical denial of Human Brotherhood. Outside the kingdom of these powers, are ignorance and inhumanity, and terror and pain; but within their realm are learning and peace, civilization and Christianity. To them let our College be dedicated, and let us glory to fill the humblest office in this service of God and man.

In this regenerative enterprise, we enlist a new auxiliary, — one which History has never yet recognized as man's moral or spiritual helpmeet in the reformation of the world;—we summon woman to the holy work of redeeming from human ills. Military and naval men speak of this or that "Arm of the National Defence." With woman at our side, we can speak of the Heart, not less than of the Head, as a source of human improvement; of inspiring youth with purer sentiments, as well as of instructing them in richer lore, and of infusing a subtler and a diviner essence into all the elements that go to make up the Body-politic, or the mystic body of Christ.

I am aware that, in proposing to educate males and females together, and to confer equal opportunities for culture upon both, we encounter some objections, — objections all the more entitled to our consideration, because they are made by pure-minded persons, and originate in a most laudable vigilance to conserve the relations of delicacy and purity between the sexes. If I do not respect the objections, I respect the motive that prompts them. It forces into review most grave and momentous considerations; and notwithstanding the novelty of the theme in an Inaugural Address, and the proneness which the frivolous-minded may have to treat it with levity, yet I propose to meet it here, in this public manner, fairly and fully, face to face, and "try conclusions" with it.

That female education should be rescued from its present reproach of inferiority, and advanced to an equality with that of males, is a conviction which has already taken fast hold of the best minds in society, and is soon to mark the grand distinction between cultivated and uncultivated communities. But those who feel the necessity of this reform may still object to congregating both sexes in the same institutions of learning. To this objection, I consider it to be a complete answer, at least for many years to come, that, as separate institutions for the different sexes would nearly double all primary outlays and current expenditures, the plan would impoverish all; and the attempt to give an equal education to both sexes, by such means, would result in bringing male education down to the present level of female education, instead of carrying the latter up to the height of the former. For the present then, if not always, the only practicable way of securing the great end of high female education, is to educate both sexes at the same seats of learning.

And here I maintain that, with such architectural arrangements as we have devised, and with such social regulations as we contemplate, young men and young women will be brought together under auspices more favorable for the inculcation and growth of those sentiments which adorn and ennoble both sexes, and fit them for the pure and exalted relations of subsequent life, than are now enjoyed in the best circles, either in city or in country.

In the first place, what I may call an architectural guardianship is constantly supplied, in the incommunicable separation of our dormitory buildings for the respective sexes, from each other. To this will be added the guardianship of a code of regulations, assigning time and place for such social meetings or visitations as propriety not merely allows but approves; and all this will be overwatched by the vigilance of a College Faculty, hardly less responsible, and I trust, hardly less heedful of the well-being of their charge than parental solicitude itself.

It is more than desirable that a certain degree of social intercourse should subsist between those who have ceased to be children, but are not yet men and women. Without such intercourse, the manners grow rude and awkward, the sentiments grow coarse and impure. How painfully this is illustrated in the life of sailors, soldiers and pioneers. In education, the problem is, to facilitate this appropriate degree of intercourse while avoiding all dangerous or indecorous familiarity. And where else, better than under the conditions I have named, can all that is desirable be promoted, and all that is perilous be shunned?

That, occasionally, an undesirable intimacy or attachment may spring up here, is not impossible. Still, I think we shall possess two antidotes against that epidemic of incongruous matches which now afflicts society both in city and country. Within the circles of fashionable city life, it is well known that young men and young women, beyond the range of cousins or immediate family relations, rarely see each other, except when the every-day guise is off and some holiday guise is on. On such occasions, the manners and the appearance, not to say the topics of conversation even, are, like the dress that is worn, studiously prepared for the occasion;—so incrusted and rigid with conventionalism, that any specimen of native simplicity or ingenuousness is recognized as a wonder, and is designated by a technical name. The doll-shop is as fit a place for studying character, as the fashionable dinner-party, the assembly, or the ball-room. The solid attainments of the mind, the enduring attractions of the heart, have there but little scope; and an iron routine holds passion and propensity in abeyance for the hour. Such spectacles, or, at least, such theatres for a kind of public display, afford no opportunity for learning either those natural dispositions or those cultivated adaptations, which constitute indispensable ingredients in the happiness of connubial life. Yet it is here, and often here only, that men, the shrewdest in their worldly dealings, make the most solemn of contracts on the lightest of considerations; and, in selecting a companion for life, employ the senses and passions, as proxies for the understanding and heart.

In sparsely-populated rural districts, the circumstances are very different, but hardly less adverse to the formation of happy marriages. There, the circle of acquaintance is so limited and each sex sees so few of the other sex, that, although the greater freedom of intercourse favors a far more intimate knowledge of character, yet there is no variety or assortment from which a congenial selection can be made. They are like customers at a meagre market, who buy what they do not want, through lack of finding what they need.* Further acquaintance with the world discovers more congenial dispositions, or tastes better suited to each other; but this is after that fatal mistake has been consummated, which never permits rectification.

On the other hand, a well-filled school assembles together a great variety of character; and a class-room, where the sexes recite in presence of each other, daily and for years, affords opportunities for a kind of acquaintance, infinitely superior to any that can ever be enjoyed, at Washington, at watering-places, or other matrimonial bazaars. For the exercise and manifes-

---

* "And I am wedding to an honorable house," said Dumbiedikes, "the Laird of Lickpelf's youngest daughter,—*she sits next us in the kirk, and that's the way I came to think on't.*"—*The Heart of Mid-Lothian, Vol. 2, Ch. XVIII.*

tation of mental capacities and attainments, there is no reception-room like the recitation-room. Here too, there will be a daily observation of manners and appearance which either are a habit, or must become habitual, through practice. Dispositions will here be subjected to the severest trials; and unworthy passions, though hidden beneath the last folds of the heart, will be roused to a shameful exposure by excitement, or stifled into extinction by the divine discipline of conscience. If to all this be added social interviews, at appropriate seasons, under guardian watchfulness and through a period of years, whatever errors of opinion may have been formed in the class-room can hardly fail to be rectified by views of other phases of character taken from these different points of observation. And when, in addition to all this, it is known that no precocious attachment that may spring up, can be consummated, until after the college life is completed, without forfeiting all connection with the college itself; and all these salutary arrangements are reinforced and corroborated by the parental counsels of the College Government, I ask whether there be any situation in life where the proprieties and the restraints, which belong to the social intercourse of the sexes, will be or can be better balanced or adjusted than here? I confidently ask, whether there be any situation in life, where the truly sacred, (though often horribly profaned,) principles and instincts which give birth and sanctity to the conjugal relation, will be likely to be better understood and guarded from harm; or will promise, in after-life, a richer amount of that bliss which God reserves as the special reward of a wise and virtuous wedlock?

Besides and beyond all this: I believe that the daily and thrice daily meetings of the sexes, with occasional interviews in social circles, will be mutually advantageous to them. It will work both moral restraint and intellectual excitement. That innate regard which each sex has for the other sex, over and above what it has for the same good qualities in its own,—the difference between friendship and love,—is too precious and too powerful an agency to be thrown away in the education of either. I believe it to be an agency which God meant we should make use of to promote the refinement, the progress and the elevation of them both. I believe it may be made to supersede many of our present coarse and crude instruments of discipline,—the goads and bludgeons of punishment which are now employed to rouse young men from the stupefaction of idleness, or beat them back from the gateways of sin.

And what a state of society does it invincibly argue, among parents, and in the community at large, if young men and young women cannot be brought together to pursue those ennobling studies and to receive those apt instructions which pre-eminently fit them for the highest duties of their common life, without mutual peril! And where in reason or in the divine commands, is there either warrant or pretext for the doctrine, that those whom God mingles together in the family, by birth; and whom, through the sacred ordinance of marriage, He designs for a still closer relation in after-life; where, I ask, is there any authority human or divine, for seizing and violently separating these same parties, for four or six or ten of the middle years of their existence?—those very years when they can best prepare themselves, by the elevation of whatever is in them of good and the suppression of whatever is in them of evil, for a future companionship so intimate as to be lost in identity. Such separation is obviously unnatural, and if it be necessary for the preservation of sexual purity, it is time that the whole community should take the alarm and hasten to devise a less monstrous remedy.

In the songs of thanksgiving which rise to heaven from all our colleges and higher schools, shall there be none but male voices in one place, and none but female voices in another?

I have now, my friends, sketched the great necessities of a race like ours, in a world like ours: A Body, grown from its elemental beginning, in health; compacted with strength and vital with activity in every part; impassive to heat and cold, and victorious over the vicissitudes of seasons and zones; not crippled by disease nor stricken down by early death; not shrinking from bravest effort, but panting, like fleetest runner, less for the prize than for the joy of the race; and rejuvenant amid the frosts of age. A Mind, as strong for the immortal as is the body for the mortal life; alike enlightened by the wisdom and beaconed by the errors of the past; through intelligence of the laws of nature, guiding her elemental forces, as it directs the limbs of its own body through the nerves of motion, thus making alliance with the exhaustless forces of nature for its strength and clothing itself with her endless charms for its beauty, and, wherever it goes, carrying a sun in its hand with which to explore the realms of nature, and reveal her yet hidden truths. And then a Moral Nature, presiding like a divinity over the whole, banishing sorrow and pain, gathering in earthly joys and immortal hopes, and transfigured and rapt by the sovereign and sublime aspiration TO KNOW AND DO THE WILL OF GOD.

Man, considered as a being of appetites and passions only, is the fellest creation that ever bestialized the earth. No Saurian or Megatherium of the monster-ëras could ever inspire such horror or disgust as he. Though powerless towards whatever is beyond the length of his destructive arm or the effluvia of his noisome breath, he is ruin and corruption to all within their reach. His senses are his only soul. Prone, immane, obscene, he crawls, like the serpent, for his prey, and wallows in bloody filth for his pastime. Greedy and gluttonous, it is only with gory fauces and maw full-gorged, that he is ever at peace. His language never rises above the guttural ejaculations of rage, or the amorous cry of concupiscence. To him belongs neither memory nor prophecy; for, of all the past he never thinks, and of all the future he never recks, and present sensations are his only heaven and hell. To all the wonders of the earth below, to the miraculous glories of the heavens above, he is blind; to all the symphonies, the sanctities and the loves of social existence he has but the adder's ear and the tiger's heart, and towards God, he is an unconscious atheist. His history is in three words: Birth, Sensation, Death! As a being of appetites and passions, man looks downward.

But behold the miracle of change wrought by Intellect in the aforetime beast. Raising his head from the earth, he looks before and after. As visions of beauty begin to form in his mind and to float before his eyes, he paws himself out from his elemental earth, gathers in his vagrant limbs, sloughs off his scaly integuments, moulds his form into symmetry and apparels it with light; though, as yet, it is only marble symmetry and icy radiance. The athletism of the Beastly man was in his limbs, but that of the Intellectual man is in his brain; and, maddened by the love of power and the demonism of pride, he educates himself to all the atrocities and insanities of ambition. His inventive and constructive faculties expend themselves in forging weapons for the petty murders of private revenge, or the multitudinous murders of war. He launches destruction further than the thunder-cloud, and the earthquake visits cities less terribly than he. With armies upon the land and with navies upon the deep, he slaughters myriads more numerous than the hosts of Sennacherib, or he swallows them in the flood of hi wrath, as the Egyptians were swallowed in the Red Sea. See now too, how the monosyllabic speech of the brute amplifies into all the phases of the human will; how words play for the despot the part of a mighty sorcerer,—now hiding themselves in secret edict or decretal to fly to distant lands, where they suddenly start up into giants for strength and fiends for malice, or are transformed into prisons and assassinations, into massacre and the excommunication of souls;—now taking on permanence in codes of law, so that the ambition of the tyrant lives to curse, for centuries after his body is dead;—and now, assuming to be oracles from God and creeds for human belief, they go forth to darken the land and the sky for ages with their bloody idolatries and woe. As a beast, man could only drink human gore, and his thirst was sometimes slaked; but, as a conqueror, he makes swimming lakes of blood for his Baiæ, and pours it out in rivers on which he sails in magnificent barges with voluptuous Cleopatras at his side. As he grows luxurious, he distils his nectar from human hearts, and nations are consumed to make incense for his pride. If he fears that a competitor for his throne is somewhere born, to destroy that one infant rival, he kills all children under two years of age,—the red margin of his fears!

He rapes Sabine women, crowds seraglios, sanctifies polygamy, erects Bastiles, devises the agonizing enginery of the Inquisition, and studies the physiology of the human frame to learn the science of torture. He invades other hemispheres, descending in whirlwind and fire upon unsuspecting Africa to carry her sons and daughters across half the earth into hells of bondage; makes Siberia populous with exiles, and colonizes Australia with the supernumeraries in his terrible census of crime. By forbidding education, he intercepts truth as it showers down from God, lest its divine power should emancipate and redeem; and thus he draws a pall of moral blackness over Italy, over Ireland and over every land of slaves. He miseducates by lying forgeries and pretended oracles of God, till nations dwarf and bestialize under the horrors of superstition, and the fatness of the earth is changed by ignorance and error into famine and death. If Art solicits the conqueror's pride, he commands it to fill his Louvres and his Vaticans with pictures whose pigments were made from human gore; and Sculpture builds his monumental pyramids of human bones, and he trains the ear of childhood to love the fiendish music of war. He walls out the all-welcoming heaven on every side, save where he sits at his own narrow wicket; and there, for the payment of money or the surrender of virtue, he sells admission to OUR Father in Heaven. The Bestial man looks downward, but when Intellect is developed, he looks around and afar.

But man, as a Moral Being, receives the anointing of virtue and religion. No longer does he call his fellow-man Jew or Gentile, Greek or barbarian, bond or free. Children of a common Father, — *brethren are they all.* The murderous steel he before clenched in his hand turns to the green olive-branch. His eye streams at the sight of woe. His heart makes others sufferings his own. No longer is it the base pride of nations to boast with how many fighting-men they can reap the harvests of death, or with what wrecks of proud navies they have inlaid the bottom of the sea; but man, risen to the consciousness of his glorious nature, now explores the world for mercy as he once explored it for gold, carrying bread where there is want, knowledge where there is ignorance, and Christian light to those who sit in the region and shadow of death. The unhallowed intellect created martial epics that wrapt the earth in the lurid fires of war; but Christian epics will help to apparel the world in the celestial light of peace. The regenerated race will do better than

to found Schools for the Orphan, or Hospitals for the Insane, or Redemption-houses for the vicious; for by following the Eternal Laws of Health, Truth and Duty, — that is *by knowing and obeying the laws of God*,—they will forestall and prevent the calamities of orphanage, insanity and crime. In that day, the cradle-song of infancy will be "Love to God and love to man," rising with age, into lofty anthems of intelligent gratitude and joy, to find its full diapason in those glories of a future life which eye hath not seen, nor ear heard, neither hath it entered into the heart of man to conceive. As I said before, the Bestial man looks earthward, and the Intellectual man looks around, but the Christian man looks heavenward, and, as he gazes, soars.

And lo! at that exalted and radiant point of man's history, when the ideas of civil and religious freedom, and an education for ALL have been secured, Woman stands by his side;—not Amazonian but angelic; gentle, yet godlike in works of knowledge and duty; meek, yet mighty in all the miracles of charity and benevolence; assuaging the wounds of humanity with a hand that touch of coarse or bloody weapons never hardened nor stained, while her heart burns like a seraph's to restore the beauties of Paradise to earth, and to usher in the era of millennial holiness and peace.

www.ingramcontent.com/pod-product-compliance
Lightning Source LLC
LaVergne TN
LVHW021417110826
845150LV00007B/1963

* 9 7 8 1 4 2 5 5 0 9 4 3 9 *